Also by Irene J. Dumas

Veterans and Still Rollin
A Salute to Our Veterans
**Vignettes of Those Who Made the Difference
1939 – 2000**
A Salute to Our Veterans
**Vignettes of the CAN-DO Navy Seabee
1942 -2007**
A Salute to Our Veterans
**Vignettes of Those Who Served Side-by-Side
For our American Freedom—1918-2007**

CENTURY'S
—— OF ——
WAR'S

IRENE J. DUMAS

Order this book online at www.trafford.com
or email orders@trafford.com

Most Trafford titles are also available at major online book retailers.

© Copyright 2020 Irene J. Dumas.

All rights reserved. No part of this publication may be reproduced, stored in a retrieval system, or transmitted, in any form or by any means, electronic, mechanical, photocopying, recording, or otherwise, without the written prior permission of the author.

Print information available on the last page.

ISBN: 978-1-6987-0061-8 (sc)
ISBN: 978-1-6987-0063-2 (hc)
ISBN: 978-1-6987-0062-5 (e)

Library of Congress Control Number: 2020907392

Because of the dynamic nature of the Internet, any web addresses or links contained in this book may have changed since publication and may no longer be valid. The views expressed in this work are solely those of the author and do not necessarily reflect the views of the publisher, and the publisher hereby disclaims any responsibility for them.

Any people depicted in stock imagery provided by Getty Images are models, and such images are being used for illustrative purposes only.
Certain stock imagery © Getty Images.

Trafford rev. 04/25/2020

 www.trafford.com

North America & international
toll-free: 1 888 232 4444 (USA & Canada)
fax: 812 355 4082

DEDICATION

This book is dedicated to those veterans that gave their last breath on battlefields and ocean waters to preserve our country's American Freedom.

This book is also dedicated to all the veterans that are here with us today and suffer from the wounds/scars that they incurred while fighting for our American Freedom.

And this book is also dedicated to our veterans that returned from wars and are still able to stand tall and are among us, they are the breath and backbone of our American Freedom, today and always.

We Salute You One and All. God Bless You and God Bless Our America

Irene Jean Dumas-Gammon

Lakeland, Florida

ACKNOWLEDGEMENTS

I want to extend my deepest appreciation to my dear niece Kristin Sirak of Hamilton, New Jersey for all her special attention in the editing of and being my best critic in keeping me on track while writing "Century's of War's".

My #1 Son Artist, William Hay, is credited for the "Art" work on the dust cover and all the drawings of "hat's" at the beginnings of the chapters. And I want to thank him for all his patience and endurance while waiting for me to decide how to bring this book to a close.

And second to none, my husband Kenneth D. Gammon gets my whole-hearted thanks and appreciation for putting up with my passion for writing and helping me by proof-reading every word.

Irene J. Dumas-Gammon
Lakeland Florida

CONTENTS

Prologue xi

Chapter 1   England 1500's 1
Chapter 2   England 1600's 6
Chapter 3   American Revolution War 10
Chapter 4   Intermediate Wars 17
Chapter 5   United States Civil War 20
Chapter 6   World War One 31
Chapter 7   World War Two 44
Chapter 8   Bombing of Pearl Harbor 49
Chapter 9   "Do You Know" 89
Chapter 10   The Korean War 91
Chapter 11   The Vietnam War 101
Chapter 12   Americans come Home from Vietnam 126
Chapter 13   Lebanon – 1982-1983 128
Chapter 14   Grenada 130
Chapter 15   Panama – 1989-90 132
Chapter 16   The Gulf War 134
Chapter 17   September 11, 2001-9/11 146
Chapter 18   Afghanistan 150
Chapter 19   Second Iraqi War 153
Chapter 20   Iraq's Beginning Civiliazation 161

Sources 165
Index 167

PROLOGUE

As an American, I am proud of my country and its many heroes that have contributed toward the making of America, the greatest country in the world. I have always had a passion for American History and even a greater passion for Military History.

Perhaps the reason is in view of the fact that my Uncle Carl Reid was a World War Two Soldier and a prisoner of war (POW) in a Nazi Concentration camp, (Stalag Five), for two years, to this day he will not talk about it.

My first husband William was in the United States Marine Corps, and fought in the Korean War, he was with the First Marine Division; unfortunately he passed away in 1992, from cancer. Two of my sons were also in the United States Marines, during peacetime and currently, I have a grandson serving in the United States Marine Corps.

I am now married to a veteran of the United States Navy Seabees (the Constructions Battalions of the Navy), my second husband Kenneth Douglas Gammon, was an officer who served as a Company Commander during the Vietnam War and retired from the United States Navy after serving for twenty-two years plus in the military.

Also, I have interviewed about one-hundred and eighty veterans from all the branches of the United States military and the British Royal Navy, and had their military careers published in three volumes titled "A Salute to Our Veterans" with different subtitles.

As I quickly focus my eyes around my study, my library of military books consists of over three hundred collections, and I have read almost all of them. Scarily a day passes that I am not reading, researching, or watching some military material. I find that in my readings that most of the stories are the same, although there are some exceptions, as to the when and where.

Here in some semblance I have written some of the history of our military, the United States military, its wars, and a few of its heroes, also a bit of military and wars from the British, before we became a nation, our own America.

CHAPTER ONE

ENGLAND 1500'S

In English, the first known use of the word military, spelled (militaries) was in 1595. It comes from Latin militaries; Latin miles meaning "soldier" but is of uncertain etymology (derivation, word history), one suggestion is of being in body or mass.

The word military is identified as denoting someone that is skilled in use of weapons, or engaged in military service or in warfare.

As a noun, "the military" usually refers to a country's Armed Forces.

Armed Forces are authorized to use deadly force and weapons to support the interests of a country, state and some or all of its citizens. The defense of the country, state and its citizens is the task of the military, and the prosecution of war against another state or country.

The military may also have additionally sanctioned and non-sanctioned functions within a society, including: the promotion of a political agenda, protecting corporate economic interests, internal population control, construction, emergency services and social affairs.

Although Wikipedia has listed wars as far back as the Norman Conquest that was from 999 to 1139, and fought in Southern Italy, in this volume I will only go back as far as the 1500's.

Back in the 1500's, the United States was unheard of. Even now we are only two centuries old, while other countries around the globe are hundreds of centuries old. During the times of the 1500's we were not even considered colonies. It wasn't until the 1600's that the first colony in the America's was established by England and under British rule.

In 1585 the word military is first known during the Anglo-Spanish War. In August of that year England joined the "Eighty-Years War", on the side of the Dutch Protestant-United Provinces, who had declared their independence from Spain. Opposing Monarchs were Phillip of Spain and Elizabeth I of England.

Causes for the war were that in the 1560s Phillip II of Spain was defending the Catholic Church in attempt to suppress the rising Protestant heresy.

At the same time, Elizabeth I of England signed "The Treaty of Nonsuch" with the Dutch rebels, agreeing to supply them with arms. Phillip took this to be an open declaration of war against his rule in the Netherlands.

In view of the fact that I am writing about the military wars fought and why they were, I feel that it is also more interesting to learn about some of the heroes during each century that the wars were fought. Below is a brief history of one that fought during the 1500's, and had a very interesting career in warfare.

Was born in Tavistock, Devon, England, between 1541 and 1544 (the uncertainty of his birth date is due to the fact that very little records were kept back then). He was the oldest of twelve sons, of Edmund Drake (1518-1585). Sir Francis Drake was an Explorer, Soldier, Slaver, Politician, and to the Spanish, a Pirate.

During the Elizabethan era Drake was the second ever to circumnavigate the world, and the first Englishmen to do so. Drake's exports were so grand that England regarded him as a hero. Queen Elizabeth I knighted him when he returned in 1581.

At the age of twelve, Francis Drake started his merchandising career. Drake's father apprenticed him to a neighbor, the shipmaster of a barge used for coastal trade that transported merchandise to France. Drake's shipmaster was so impressed with his skills and conduct, that upon the shipmasters death and being unmarried and childless he left the barge to Drake. This showed that Drake was a skilled sailor even in his youth. After selling the ship, Drake sailed to Devon to sail with his relative John Hawkins.

In 1567, Drake made one of the first voyages with Hawkins bringing slaves to the new world. During the voyage, all but two of the ships were lost when attacked by a Spanish squadron. After which the Spanish became a lifelong enemy for Drake.

While home from one of many voyages, Drake met and fell in love with Mary Newman. On the 4th day of July 1569, Francis Drake married Mary at St Budeaux church. St. Budeaux was a Devon country parish, four miles from Plymouth. After their marriage, they lived in Plymouth. The couple never had any children, probably because Drake spent most of his time on voyages.

In 1572, Queen Elizabeth I commissioned Drake to sail as a privateer to the Americas. In its first raid, Drake and his men captured the town and its treasure. During that raid, a bullet hit and injured Drake in the battle and his men left the treasure to save his life; but determined to catch treasure shipment Drake stayed in the area for almost a year, fortunately, for him throughout the year he kept low and was not captured.

In 1573, he joined a French buccaneer to attack a rich Spanish mule train at Nombre de Dios. Drake and his party captured around twenty tons of silver and gold. When they arrived back to where they left their raiding boats, all the boats were gone. They buried the treasure, built a raft, and Drake with two of his men sailed back to the Flagship.

By August 1573, he returned to England with a Spanish treasure and a reputation as a brilliant privateer, and once again commissioned by the Queen. The Queen wanted Drake to undertake an expedition to the Pacific Coast of the Americas to disrupt Spanish supply lines. In order that the voyage might be successful, all orders given were of classified nature and the crews on all five ships sworn to secrecy.

Due to bad weather, before they were able to reach the Pacific, all that remained was his Flagship, the Golden Hine, the only ship that continued the voyage. Drake sailed north along the West Coast of South America attacking ships and towns. During this time, he captured a heavy load of gold, wine and treasures.

In June 1579, Drake landed somewhere north of Spain's northern most plains. He repaired and restocked his vessels, keeping friendly relations with the natives. Drake headed across the Pacific and reached a group of islands in the South West; he sailed along the tip of Africa, then around the tip of Cape Good Hope and returned home in September 1580. Drake in his Golden Hind sailed into Plymouth with his remaining crew of 59 aboard, along with a large cargo of rich spices and captured Spanish treasures. At that time, Drake became known as the first Englishman to circumnavigate the Earth and the second such voyage arriving with at least one ship intact.

In April 1581 Queen Elizabeth 1, awarded Drake Knighthood aboard the Golden Hind. Drakes wife Mary became Lady Drake. In addition, in 1581, Drake became the Mayor of Plymouth for a term of 12 months and Mary was the mayoress. Francis and Mary Drake did not have any children. Also in 1582, the Drake's acquired Buckland Abbey, a mansion in the Devon parish of Buckland Monachorum, north of Plymouth. Unfortunately, Mary Drake did not enjoy the status for very long, in January 1583, she passed away.

In 1585, Drake again married, his second wife's name was Elizabeth Sydenham, born 1562, the only child of Sir George Sydenham, of Combe Sydenham. Elizabeth and Francis Drake also never had any children. Soon after the marriage, war began to break out between Spain and England in 1585. The Queen through Francis Walsingham ordered Sir Francis Drake to lead an expedition to attack the Spanish. An expedition left Plymouth in September 1585, with Drake in command of twenty-one ships and 1,800 soldiers.

The first attack was at Vigo in Spain, and then came an attack at Santiago in the Cape Verde Islands, after which the fleet sailed across the Atlantic, sacked the port of Santo Domingo, and captured the city of Cartagena de Indies in present-day-Colombia. On 6 June 1586 while returning home, the voyage raided the Spanish Fort of San Augustine in Spanish Florida.

After the raids the warriors then went on to find Sir Walter Raleigh's settlement much further north in the Americas, at Roanoke. They replenished and took back with them all the original colonists before Sir Richard Greynvil, and when they sailed into Portsmouth, England was given a hero's welcome.

Sir Frances Drake continued sailing into his mid-fifties, in 1595 Drake lost a series of battles against the Spanish and the new world. During a battle the Spanish shot a cannon ball through Drakes cabin, although he survived Sir Francis died a few weeks later of dysentery at age 56.

Sir Francis Drake's burial was at sea in a lead coffin and dressed in full cloth and full armor. It is implied that his final resting place is near the wrecks of two British ships, the Elizabeth and the Delight, scuttled in Portobello Bay. Divers continue to search for the coffin. After Drakes death, his widow Elizabeth eventually married Sir William Courtenay of Powderham.

In this period the Spanish were able to refit and retool their navy, the pride of the fleet was named, "The Twelve Apostles", twelve on the Spanish treasure fleet during the 1590s.

CHAPTER TWO

ENGLAND 1600'S

After several years of war between Spain and England, the Treaty of London in 1604 stored the status. The protestant reformation in England now protected, and James and his ministers refused the Spanish demand for Catholic totalitarian in England. English supports for the Dutch rebellion against the Spanish king, the original causes of the war ended.

Queen Elizabeth died around 1603, the new king of England was James 1, the Protestant son and successor of the Catholic Mary, Queen of Scott, whose execution had been the approximate cause of the war. James regarded himself as the peacemaker of Europe and the ultimate aim of his idealistic foreign policy was the reunion of Christendom. Therefore, when James came to the English throne, his first order of business was to negotiate peace with Phillip III of Spain, who had succeeded Phillip II. An end came with a treaty in 1648 when the Dutch Republic had been recognized as an independent country.

For this century my chosen warrior is someone whose name appeared quite frequently, because he had a long career in the military during the 1600's and those eras wars are Count of Tilley, Johann Yserclaes.

Johann Yserclaes, Count of Tilley, was born in February 1559 in Castle Tilley, Walloon Brabant, and now Belgium. He was born into a Roman Catholic family; after receiving a Jesuit education in Cologne, he joined the Spanish Army at age fifteen. Johann fought under the Duke of Parma in the Eighty Years' War and a successful Siege of Antwerp in1585. After this, he joined the Holy Roman Empire's campaign as a mercenary and became a field marshal in five years. He remained in the service in Prague until his appointment as commander of the Catholic League Forces by Bavaria under Maximilian I. (Tilley), as Commander of the forces of the Catholic

League, fought on 8 November 1620, the Battle of White Mountain, west of Prague; against Christian of Anhalt and Count Thurn. With the force of 25,000 soldiers, including troops of both the Catholic League and the Emperor, they scored an important victory.

At the end of April 1622, Count Tilley was defeated at the Battle of Mingolsheim. Once awarded the title of Count Tilley there was no stopping the "Monk in armor" Johann Tserclaes.

His campaigns included: being involved in the Eighty Years' War, Fall of Antwerp, Long Turkish War, Thirty Years' War, Battle of White Mountain (1620), Battle of Mingolsheim (1622), Battle of Wimpfen(1622), Battle of Hochst (1622), Seige of Heidelberg (1622), Capture of Mannheim (1622) Battle of Stadtlohn (1623), Battle of Lutter (1626), and Sack of Magdeburg (1631).

The Protestant city of Magdeburg, a battle causing the death of about 20,000 of the cities inhabitants, both defenders and civilians, out of a total of 25,000. Count Tilley, was then crushed at Breitenfeld in 1631 by the Swedish Army. He had been hit by a Swedish cannonball in the battle of Rain and died fifteen days later of tetanus at the age of 73 on 30 April 1632.

During and after the above time, other hostilities or wars were taking place.

1602 – 1663 - Dutch Portuguese War

1635 – 1659 – Franco-Spanish War

1640 – 1701 – Beaver Wars also known as the Iroquois Wars or the French and Iroquois Wars 17th Century in Eastern North America was fought over fur trade. The Iroquois Confederation led by the dominant Mohawk, against the Algonquian-speaking tribes of the Great

Lakes Region. The Iroquois were armed by the Dutch and English trading partners, the Algonquian backed by the French.

On 4 July 1675-Aug. 1676-King Philip's War...New England Colonies vs. Wampanoag, Narragansett, and Nipmuck Indians

1689-1697 – King William's War... English Colonies vs. France

The 1700's has brought with it another series of wars, some are listed below:

1702 – 1713 – Queen Anne's War (War of Spanish Succession)....The English Colonies vs. France

1744 - 1748 – King George's War (War of Austrian Succession)....The French Colonies vs. Great Britain

1756-1763 - French and Indian War (Seven Years War)....The French Colonies vs. Great Britain

1759-1761 – Cherokee War....English Colonies vs. Cherokee Indians

The wars were brutal and considered one of the bloodiest series in the history of North America. The Iroquois destroyed several tribal confederacies, including Huron, Neutral, Erie, Susquenhannock and Shawnee as they were realigning the tribal geography of North America. They pushed some eastern tribes to the West of the Mississippi River, or Southward into the Carolinas gaining control of the Ohio Valley hunting lands from 1670 onward. The Ohio country and Lower Peninsula of Michigan became empty of Native people as refugees fled westward to escape the Iroquois warriors. The English used the Iroquois conquests as a claim to the Old Northwest Territory.

Although I will not list them all, there were many other small conflicts and wars happening between the years 1701 and 1754 when the French and Indian War was fought between France and Spain on one side and Great Britain on the other side. Ending in 1754 and resulting in the Brits conquest of all of New France east of the Mississippi River, as well as Spanish Florida.

The outcome was France's colonial presence north of the Caribbean was reduced to the tiny islands of Saint Pierre and Miquelon. Spain lost Florida, and France ceded its control of French Louisiana west of the Mississippi.

CHAPTER THREE

AMERICAN REVOLUTION WAR

1775-1783 – American Revolution….English Colonies vs. Great Britain

The American Revolutionary War also known as the American War of Independence, began as a war between the Kingdom of Great Britain and (only) thirteen British colonies on the North American continent that were chiefly governed by the British until the time of the Revolutionary War. In the nineteenth century, the United States transformed itself, from thirteen tiny colonies hugging the Eastern seaboard to a continental giant stretching from Sea to shining sea. This was fought because the thirteen colonies wanted to be independent and not be under the rule of England. Listed here are the 13 Colonies, in the order that they were established and the population of each colony at the beginning of the Revolutionary War.

Virginia/Jamestown: 1607 Jamestown was the first of the 13 colonies after the failure to establish a colony on Roanoke Island. The London Company founded it in 1607. Jamestown was founded mainly for making money. It was a port and trading center. Another reason, much less pressing than the financial aspect, was to minister to and covert the natives to Christianity.

In 1624, a larger area was named Virginia. This area encompassed Jamestown.

Massachusetts: The second colony founded was Massachusetts, in 1620. The Pilgrims formed this colony, known as the Separatists or Puritans. They came over to escape British rule. This group decided that the people should decide everything. They wanted their government to be a democracy and believed the people had the right to say what happened to them and who ruled over them, population 235,808.

New Hampshire: 1623 the land was given to John Mason, and he decided to make a colony with it. Because Mason lived in Hampshire County in England, is why the colony name is New Hampshire. He invested a lot of money in this land, making cities and towns. Sadly, he never saw it, due to his death in 1635, population 62,396.

Maryland: 1632-34 Maryland, a place founded to create a place for Roman Catholics who were still struggling against religious tyranny in England. In addition, Lord Baltimore saw an opportunity for profit, population 202,599.

Connecticut: 1635 Connecticut mostly consisted of people looking for freedom from government, people looking to earn their fortune, and people just coming to the "New World". There were also many religious people, as there were in all the colonies at that time, 183,881 citizens.

Rhode Island: 1636 the sixth colony, when Roger Williams wanted to make changes in religion in Massachusetts, the government did not take it very well. They banished him to England, but instead he went to live with the Native Americans. They formed a group and called it Providence, 58,196 population.

Later, due to religious reasons three other people had been banished, these three also left and formed small groups. These four groups requested British permission to become a colony. The King consented, thus creating Rhode Island.

Delaware: Founded in 1638, Delaware was originally of New Sweden, which also included Philadelphia and other parts of Pennsylvania. Later the king of England gained control over the portion east of the Delaware River and named it Delaware, population 35,496.

North Carolina: Founded in 1653, in 1653 some Virginians grew tired of religious laws, and moved just south of the border to start their own group. Soon after, the king granted the land as a gift to some noblemen. They sent people over to colonize the area and some of them joined with the group that was already there. At first, they called it Carolina. Later, in 1664, because of strife within the colony, the noblemen sold the land back to the crown. Eventually, it separated into two colonies, the North and the South Carolina, 197,200 population.

South Carolina: this colony formed in 1664 the same time as North Carolina, population 124,244.

New York: Founded in 1664, when the Duke of York received New Netherland as a gift, it was renamed New York in his honor. He broke off two pieces of the land allotted to him and gave them to two of his friends. These were the foundation for New Jersey, population 162,920.

New Jersey: Founded 1664, when two friends of the Duke of York received land from him, they decided to colonize it. They wanted as many people to come and live there as possible, so they began to make promises about all the different things you could gain from the New World, such as fortune and freedom, population 117,431.

Pennsylvania: Founded in 1682, it was the twelfth colony. In 1682, William Penn received land from his grandfather, who had recently passed away. Penn, a Quaker, wanted freedom of religion and protection from persecution for himself and others who might want the same thing. He had not been able to find this, so he started his own colony. He called it Pennsylvania, population 240,057.

Georgia: 1732: It was the last of the 13 colonies. James Oglethorpe asked the king for a land charter and so granted an unpopulated portion of land from the Carolina charter called Georgia, after King George. Oglethorpe had two motives for making this colony. One was for people to start new after serving time in jail, the other, to serve as a military base to defend against the Spanish, population 23,375.

The Thirteen Colonies take up arms against the mother country:
In January of 1776 the New Hampshire Gazette inquired, "**Can we gain Independency**"? The answers if accurate give a fair summery of the odds faced by the American Colonies as they took up arms against the mother country.

The Colonies started grouping together when the Americans were not being treated fairly by the Mother Country (Britain), who had authority over them.

There were many signs of British tyranny. Beyond the Proclamation and the Stamp Act, were the suppression of paper currency and the Sugar Act, all seeming to be part of a deliberate policy to curtail America's freedom and deny that liberty which was an essential right to humanity.

Sons of Liberty were making life unbearable for the British custom officials, and the British government was understandably provoked by Boston's treasonable and desperate intention against the Crown.

To protect Royal Officials in their duties to the Crown four thousand redcoats arrived in Boston Harbor during the fall of 1768. The occupation of force on a city that had already been torn with conflict only made bloodshed a predicted conclusion.

The Bostonians refused to house the soldiers, street fights where frequent, mobs taunted the troops with cries of bloody backs, while Samuel Adams and sons coup in the background, planning the flames of revolt.

The ruling of the King for placing high tax on them was frustrating; the Americans were also upset because of the Religious rule, that they were to live by.

The beginning of the real fight between the Thirteen Colonies and the British Military began on 19 April 1775.

The American Commander-in-Chief had the problem of creating an Army out of skeptical material. George Washington described his recruits as a mixed group of people, under little discipline, order or government.

No less than 395,859 American enlistments were recorded, most for a three-month enlistment service upheld by both the people and the Continental Congress Foreign nations, including France and Spain, later allied with the American colonists and the French still later declared war on Britain.

Britain had put a small army in the campaign to fight the thirteen colonies; in view of it, it was at a time when France and Spain could very well have decided to invade England.

French involvement proved decisive with a French naval victory in the Chesapeake leading to the surrender of a second British army at Yorktown in 1781.

In 1783, the Treaty of Paris ended the war among the countries, with all recognizing the sovereignty and independence of the United States within the territory bounded by what is now Canada to the north, Florida to the south and the Mississippi River to the west.

That is how we received our American Independence, our Heritage. It is hard to believe that only a group of thirteen colonies could overthrow a country as large as England. Yet they did! When the Revolutionary War started in 1776, the Colonies had a 2.5 million population and the British had 6.5-7.5 million population.

My first thought was to choose our first President, General George Washington as the 1700's outstanding American soldier, who was Commanding General to the Continental Army, and later the First President of the United States. George was an outstanding soldier and commander, he had quite an interesting military history; he was a good and courageous soldier, although after reading-up on Washington's full personal history, there was a period in his life that I felt him not so favorable to my choosing him for my 1700's special victor.

The incident that I have in mind accrued when at Washington's urging Governor Lord Botetourt fulfilled Dinwiddie's promise of land bounties to all volunteer militia during the French and Indian Wars.

In late 1770, Washington inspected the lands in the Ohio and Great Kanawha regions, and he hired surveyor William Crawford to subdivide it. Crawford allotted 23,200 acres to Washington to be distributed to the war veterans.

Washington told the veterans that their land was hilly and unsuitable for farming, and then he agreed to purchase 20,147 acres for himself, leaving some feeling that they had been deceived. He also doubled the size of Mount Vernon to 6.500 acres and increased his slave count to more than 100. Knowing all this, I quickly focused my attention to finding a more suitable soldier.

My second choice for victor was John Adams whose record was an interesting one and deserving. However, upon reading his history, found that he was not a soldier; he was a Member of Congress, a politician, one of the signers of the Declaration of Independence and the Second President of the United States.

Another warrior that I considered for my choice was that mighty fighter: Arnold Benedict of the 1700's. After digging into the annuals of war, I decided while reading about Benedict not to write his military history. Arnold when his plot to surrender West Point to the Brits was uncovered. Benedict deserted the Colonies war and fled to join the British. Nevertheless, I welcome all my readers to enjoy reading about my choice of: **Major General**  **Nathanael Greene** who was born the 7th day of August 1742, on Forge Farmat Potowomuy in the township of Warwick, Rhode Island, which was then part of British North America. He was the son of Mary Mott and Nathanael Greene Sr., a successful merchant and farmer.

Due to his religious beliefs, his father did not believe in book learning. Nevertheless Greene convinced his father to hire a tutor, he studied mathematics, the classics, law, and other works. At some point in his childhood, Nathanael acquired a limp that followed him the rest of his life.

In 1774, Greene married Catharine Littlefield, they had their first child in 1776, and they had six more children between 1777 and 1786. After his father's death Nathanael and his brothers inherited the family business.

When the French and Indian Wars ended (1754-1763), the British Upper Chamber decided it would change policies that would raise revenue from the British North Americas.

After William Dudington seized a vessel owned by Greene and his brothers. The Greene's filed a successful lawsuit against Dudington for damages. In the interim Dudington's ship had been set on fire by a Rhode Island gang. After the incident, Greene became separated from the British government.

Because of the increases of revenue on the colonies, the colonies grew angry and soon united in organizing for what everyone knew was going to be war. Greene helped organize a local military known as the Kentish Guards.

In May when Greene's column was on the march, complete with supplies, uniformed, disciplined, and including a wagon train full of artillery. In command was Nathanael Greene as they reported to General John Thomas at Roxbury. When the mainspring of the Army finally been brought into reasonable manageable shape. Nathanael Greene with his group was under the command of Charles Lee, as was John Sullivan of New Hampshire.

In June of 1775 the Second Continental Congress established the Continental Army, appointed George Washington Commander-in-Chief to the Colonial Forces, Congress also appointed six Generals, and Greene was appointed Brigadier General and was given command of seven Regiments from different colonies.

Nathanael Greene, July 27, 1742- June 19, 1786. He died at his Mulberry Grove Plantation, in Chatham County, Georgia.

The Siege of Boston continued until March when the British forces left the city. Washington established his headquarters in Manhattan and Greene had the task of preparing for the invasion of Long Island. Greene saw action at the Battle of Harlem Heights and later was placed in command of Fort Constitution (later known as Fort Lee), which was on the New Jersey side of the Hudson River. Greene commanded part of Washington's Army in December 1776 at the Battle of Trenton when Washington's Army crossed the Delaware. In January 1777, Greene with his command joined Washington at the Battle of Princeton. Both Trenton and Princeton ended in victories for the Continental Army.

Greene had been stationed in New Jersey for half of 1777, after that he fought at the Battle of Brandywine; Greene commanded a division at the center of the American line. The British captured Philadelphia after the Battle of Brandywine.

Nathanael Greene continued his military, also fighting at Germantown, Monmouth, and Springfield. It is written in history books that Greene was one of the Commander-in-Chief's most trusted lieutenants. His successful campaign is why I chose him to represent the 1700's century.

CHAPTER FOUR

INTERMEDIATE WARS

1798-1800 – Franco-American Naval War...United Sates vs. France

1801-1805; 1815 – Barbary Wars....United States vs. New Morocco, Algiers, Tunis and Tripoli

1812-1815 – War of 1812.... United States vs. Great Britain

1813-1814 – Creek War....United States vs. Creek Indians

In the year 1823, Governor Jose Antonio Vizcarra met Navajo leaders at Paguate and stated that the Spanish would settle the Navajo in pueblos and energetically convert them to the Catholic religion. The Navajo rejected the treaty and renewed the fight. Several Mexicans were killed at Socorro in April and eight more at Sabinal in May.

In June 1823 Vizcarra led 1,500 troops in a 74-day expedition against the Navajo of western New Mexico. He traveled through the Chuska Mountains to the Hopi mesas in what is now Arizona, then north towards Utah, reaching Oljeto Creek in what is now San Juan County, Utah. The expedition reached Canyon de Chelly in what is now eastern Arizona.

The 1823 raid marked the start of a long period of raids and counter raids lasting until 1848 as New Mexicans took Navajo captive to work as slaves.

1836 – War of Texas Independence....Texas vs. Mexico

1846-1848 – Mexican-American War.....United States vs. Mexico

The Mexican-American War, also known as the American intervention in Mexico was an armed conflict between the United States of America and the Second Federal Republic of Mexico. It followed in the wake of the annexation of the Republic of Texas.

In the quest for California, President Polk an advocate of war with Mexico from the beginning argued strongly for annexation, because Americans were the most numerous people in the area, and motivated by his knowledge of gold deposits there and sought British help to persuade Mexico to sell the area to the United States.

The United States military assumed nominal control of the southwest from Mexico by 1846. In addition, the raids between the Navajo and the New Mexican civilians continued.

> 1849: Washington Expedition – August 1849, the U.S. Army began an expedition into the heart of Navajo country on an organized reconnaissance to impress the Navajo with the might of the U.S. military; the expedition was led by Col. John Washington, the military governor of New Mexico.

At the end of August the expedition were in need of water, they began looting Navajo cornfields. Navajo warriors pushed them off. Washington reasoned pillage Navajo crops because the Navajo would have to reimburse the United States government for the cost of the expedition.

In spite of the situation, Washington suggested to the Navajo that they and the whites could still be friends if the Navajo came with their chiefs the next day and signed a treaty.

The next day the chief along with several headmen came to view the treaty, in the treaty the Navajo acknowledging the U.S. on its part promised "such donations (and) such other liberal and humane measures, as (it) may deem meet the proper". After reaching an accord, a shuffle broke out when a New Mexico soldier claimed he saw a Navajo on his stolen horse.

The Navajo held that the horse rightfully belonged to him. While Washington sided with the New Mexican, the Navajo owner took his horse and fled the scene, Washington told the New Mexican to pick out any Navajo horse he wanted. The rest of the Navajo also left.

Col. Washington ordered his soldiers to fire, seven Navajo Indians were shot and killed, and the rest of the Indians ran. In the volley Chief Narbona, was scalped as he lay dying by a New Mexican souvenir hunter, the massacre prompted a war.

Without food or shelter to sustain them through the winters, and continuously chased by the United States Army groups the Navajo began to surrender.

> 1851 – 1860 for several more years the Navajo and the New Mexicans fought each other then in 1862 the Civil War began. Confederate Forces advanced up the Rio Grande into New Mexico in 1862; and were driven back into Texas by Union Forces of the Colorado Volunteers and assisted by some New Mexican Volunteer militia units.

Starting in January 1864, many bands of Indians and their leaders gave-up to their Calvary or were captured and made what is called the "Long Walk" to the Bosque Redondo reservation at Fort Sumner, New Mexico.

Around December of 1864, in a theater in Denver an audience cheered as an ordained Methodist minister on stage outward showed the accomplishments of the latest clash with Indians. The Preachers name was John, and he was a volunteer preacher with the Cavalry. He had lead an attacking party to Sand Creek, Colorado, where they massacred at least one-hundred-fifty Indian children women and old men. The braves had been away from camp. What made them cheer so much is a pile of hacked Indian penises, and applauded lauder when the American soldiers displayed hats over which they had stretched vaginal skin of Indian women. Our president at the time was thought nothing wrong in even the most barbaric American actions.

CHAPTER FIVE

UNITED STATES CIVIL WAR

1861-1865 – United States Civil War....Union vs. Confederacy

As an American History fanatic, I have often wondered if the Civil War's only cause was by a disagreement of freeing the slaves. Therefore, I read and reread extensively about that period and war. My conclusion is that the Civil War was certainly all about the freeing of slaves.

One of the reasons I learned was that the south did not want to free their slaves, especially when in 1793, Yankee, Eli Whitney invented the cotton gin, a tool that the mills could use to make use of short staple cotton. In the south cotton was plentiful, its most worthy commodity for the colonies and abroad. Therefore, the cotton field proprietors used slaves for cheap labor to pick the cotton fields, and naturally wanted to keep the slaves.

The name John Brown had for many years stuck in my mind, and every time that I heard the song "John Brown Had a Little Indian" I knew that he had to have a history some place. It was not until I was reading about the Civil War that I was able to clear my thoughts up as to why I had heard that name before and it was not only due to the song.

In 1855, proslavery patrols clashed with antislavery patrols; there were barn burnings, horse stealing and shootings. The free-soil settlement had been already sacked by a proslavery mob. In retaliation, John Brown and his followers murdered five Southern settlers near Pottawatomie Creek.

John was behind the movement from the North that advertised "Freedom for all Slaves". He had considered himself God's chosen instrument to free them. He made his decision that he would head the blacks into a revolt against their masters and that would put an end to slavery.

He would strike blows against the system, he raided plantations and carried off slaves to Canada to escape. Eventually, John returned to the United States with a price over his head.

On 16 October 1859, John and seventeen followers swung down a lonely road to Harpers Ferry; to a village at the junction of the Shenandoah and the Potomac. The small regime assaulted and captured the U. S. armory and arsenal and while waiting for the slaves of the countryside to join them an alarm went off.

Volunteers and militia companies mustered regulars and marines to the scene. The attack under fire, Brown and his troops lose heavily; two of his sons had been killed.

On the morning of the 18th Commanding Officer Robert E. Lee ordered another assault, John Brown was wounded and ten of his men were killed, two escaped and five taken prisoners.

At John Brown's trial, charges for murder, treason to the Commonwealth of Virginia and conspiracy with slaves to produce insurrection; he was found guilty of all charges.

As he rose to hear his sentence John had no doubt that he would face death, yet he stood unafraid. Moreover, out of his mind and soul came a plea for the oppressed of his country that still rings with the aspiration of humanity today. Now I know why I heard about John Brown a long time ago, in a song; and yes, he is a legend.

Back in 1860 when the Presidential election was held, and due to the unrest of the states dealing with slavery, and the fact that Lincoln was a moderate on the slavery question and agreed that the Federal Government lacked power to interfere with the institution of the states, Lincoln won the election.

After it saw the returns, Charleston, South Carolina summoned a State convention that South Carolina should secede from the union. The cotton states followed, and by February 1861, Mississippi, Alabama, Georgia, Florida, Louisiana and Texas followed.

The 8th day of February, delegates from the seceding states met in Montgomery, Alabama and set up a new nation "The Confederate States of America", and voted Jefferson Davis of Mississippi as President.

The American Civil War begins - 1861-1865

The Civil War battles between the Union States and the Confederate States began for the freeing of all slaves. While the North wanted to do away with slavery, the Confederate States wanted to keep slaves. Therefore, to resolve whether the United States of America would be continuing to exist as a slaveholding country the Civil War began.

On 12 April 1861 in Charleston Bay at Fort Sumter, the Confederate Army opened fire on the Federal garrison forcing it to lower the American flag and surrender.

On 15 April President A. Lincoln called-to-arms 75,000 volunteers and offered Robert E. Lee to command the Union Army. On 19 April, Lincoln declared the seal-off of Confederate ports from S. Carolina to Texas. The following day unfortunately, Lee resigns.

In addition to the request of 15 April, on 3 May 1861 President Lincoln makes another request for 42,000 volunteers for an enlistment of three-year tour in either Army or Navy.

Queen Victoria of England announced British neutrality on the 13th of May and 10 June Napoleon II also announced neutrality.

The first battle of Bull Run was won by the confederates. There were battles in Fredericksburg, Virginia, Gettysburg, Pennsylvania, New Jersey, New York, Shiloh, Tennessee, Kentucky, Antietam, in Maryland, Vicksburg on the Mississippi to Chickamauga and Atlanta in Georgia to name a few.

Sometime later Robert E. Lee ended up on the Confederate side of the war and I found him with his Army of Northern Virginia, when they were kept at bay by attacks from the Union Army of the Potomac, commanded by several generals and finally by Ulysses S. Grant from the Western theater.

Taps: In the United States we have heard of the haunting song, "Taps". It is a song that gives most of us a lump in our throats, and tears in our eyes. It is usually played during a military funeral or event. But do you know the story behind the song? If not, I think that you would be interested to find out about its humble beginnings.

The haunting melody, we now know as "Taps"...used at military funerals was born.

The tune is a variation of an earlier bugle call known as the "Scott Tattoo", which was used in the U.S. from 1835 until 1860, and was arranged in its present form by the Union Army Brigadier General Daniel Butterfield, an American Civil War general and Medal of Honor recipient who commanded the 3rd Brigade of the 1st Division in the V Army Corps of the Army of the Potomac while at Harrison's Landing, Virginia, in July 1862 to replace a previous French bugle call used to signal "lights out". Butterfield's bugler, Oliver Wilcox Norton, of East Springfield, Pennsylvania, was the first to sound the new call. Within months "Taps" was used by both Union and Confederate forces. It was officially recognized by the United States Army in 1874.

The words are…

> Day is done…Gone the sun…From the lakes…From the hills, from the sky…All is well…Safely rest…God is nigh
>
> Fading light…Dims the sight…And a star…Gems the sky…Gleaming bright…From afar…Drawing nigh…fall the night.

The Battle of Gettysburg began July 1, 1863, at precisely 8 am that morning; the two sides were exchanging gunfire. The desperate fight waged between artillery and infantry at close range was without either side having any cover. Bullets whistling everywhere, cannon roaring, smoke, dust and blood was all indescribable, and soon the entire Union line was gone, with survivors fleeing through Gettysburg to get to high ground.

Soon the Union troops were out-numbered; and driven back to a Christian Theological Seminary building on Seminary Ridge. Eleven thousand men had been either lost as prisoners or as casualties with only about five thousand Yankees left for action on Cemetery Hill.

The second day at Gettysburg had not been any better for the Union Army. At Cemetery Hill, the Union Army braced to meet Hoods attacks across the wheat field and the peach orchard, then the rebels advanced, by evening the confederates forced a temporary break in the Unions line at Cemetery Hill.

The last day of fighting at Gettysburg a survivor recalled was terrible, a sound that no soldier ever forgets, the noise was loud and strange with wounded and killed men falling all around. Finally, the confederates withdrew.

On July 4, the heavy rain washed away the blood of many, many soldiers. For the three day battle there was 50,000 casualties from both sides.

Because of the epic proportions of the Battle of Gettysburg, the North and the South did fight it was only proper that they were given a proper cemetery. A portion of seventeen acres was set aside on Cemetery Hill for a soldier's cemetery.

During the Civil War, at Gettysburg, Pennsylvania, on 19 November 1863, President Abraham Lincoln spoke at the dedication of the Soldiers National Cemetery in Gettysburg four and a half months after the Union defeated those of the Confederacy at the Battle of Gettysburg.

The speech that President Lincoln gave at the dedication follows:

Gettysburg Address.

Four score and seven years ago our fathers brought forth on this continent, a new nation, conceived in Liberty, and dedicated to the proposition that all men are created equal.

Now we are engaged in a great civil war, testing whether that nation or any nation so conceived and so dedicated, can long endure. We are met on a great battle-field of that war. We have come to dedicate a portion of that field, as a final resting place for those who here gave their lives that that nation might live. It is altogether fitting and proper that we should do this.

But, in a larger sense, we cannot dedicate—we cannot consecrate—we cannot hallow—this ground. The brave men, living and dead, who struggled here, have consecrated it, far above our poor power to add or detract. The world will little note, nor long remember what we say here, but it can never forget what they did here. It is for us the living, rather, to be dedicated here to the unfinished work which they who fought here have thus far so nobly advanced. It is rather for us to be here dedicated to the great task remaining before us—that from these honored dead we take increased devotion to that cause for which they gave the last full measure of devotion—that we here highly resolve that these dead shall not have died in vain—that this nation, under God, shall have a new birth of freedom—and that government of the people, by the people, for the people, shall not perish from the earth.

Several battles including Spotsylvania, Cold Harbor, the Wilderness, and Petersburg were fought until General Grant finally was able to bring Lee to bay at Appomattox on 1 April 1865. During this time, other battles were going on in the Appalachian Mountain chain and General William Tecumseh Sherman led his army deep into the Confederate heartland of Georgia and South Carolina. All the while General George Thomas destroyed the Confederacy's Army of Tennessee at the battle of Nashville.

On 4th March 1865, President Abraham Lincoln is inaugurated for a second term.

Civil government is once again restored in Tennessee, when on the second day of April the confederates move out of Richmond.

President Lincoln was at Fords Theater in Washington D. C. on 14 of April when shots rung out and hit him, John Wilkes Booth shot Lincoln, the next day Lincoln died and Andrew Johnson became the next President.

On the 26th of April, President Johnson accepts from Sherman the same surrender terms Grant offered Lee. On that same day, John Wilkes Booth is killed by Federal cavalry near Bowling Green, Virginia.

The Civil War ended on 26 May, 1865.

On a warm spring day in May 1865, the Union cavalry captured and killed the Confederate President, Jefferson Davis in Georgia.

The Northern victory preserved the United States as one nation and ended the institution of slavery that had divided the country from its beginning.

Andersonville, plus other Confederate War Prisons: After the war ended thousands of recently released Union prisoners of war that had been held by the Confederacy at the prison camps of Cahaba near Selma, Alabama and Andersonville in Southwest Georgia, had been brought to a small parole camp outside of Vicksburg to await release to the North.

The paroled soldiers were from primarily the states of Ohio, Michigan, Indiana, Tennessee and West Virginia. They boarded the steamship Sultana. The steamship was supposed to be waiting for a replacement of a ruptured seam. Because the captain did not want to wait for a delay to make the repair, he asked the mechanic to fix it temporarily so that the soldiers could be on their way home.

The steamboat only had a legal capacity of only 376 people, but by the time the ship backed away from Vicksburg on 24 April 1865 she was severely overcrowded with 1,960 paroled prisoners, 22 guards, 70 paying cabin passengers and 85 crew members, a total of 2,137 people. The men were packed into every available space, and the overflow was so severe that in some places, the decks began to crack and sag and had to be supported with heavy wooden beams. Near 2:00 A.M., on 27 April 1865 when the Sultana was just seven miles North of Memphis, her boilers suddenly exploded. First one boiler exploded, followed a split second later by two more. The exact death toll is unknown, although the most recent evidence indicates 1,168.

On 19 May 1865, less than a month after the disaster, Brig. Gen. Hoffman, Commissary General of the Prisoners, who investigated the disaster, reported an overall loss of soldiers, passengers, and crew of 1, 238.

The American Civil War had cost the lives of 625,000; it was the largest and most destructive war in the Western world between the end of the Napoleonic Wars in 1815 and the onset of World War I in 1914.

Because he grabbed my attention so many times while I researched the history of the Civil War, I have included American soldier, politician, humanitarian, equestrian, and President, Ulysses S. Grants military history for the next few pages of my book.

Ulysses S. Grant (born Hiram Ulysses Grant) April 27, 1822-July 23, 1885.

From his early childhood in Ohio, Grant had been trained to the taming of horses. He was a graduate of West Point in 1843 and served in the Mexican-American War. After the war, Grant married Julia Dent and they had four children.

Grant resigned from the army in 1854 and for the next seven years lived a civilian lifestyle. Then in 1861 when the Civil War broke out, he enlisted into the Union Army and due to his experience while serving in the previous war Lincoln promoted Grant to General early in his enlistment.

Assigned to the unruly 21 Illinois Volunteer Regiment, Grant had his hands full, finally after restoring the regiment to order the regiment was transferred to Missouri. The governor of Illinois wanted to send the troops off in railroad cars, the soldiers said that they were not going the 100 miles in boxcars that were dirty. Grant told them that if they did not want to travel in freight cars that they could walk the 100 miles, in fact, the commander thought that it would be good training for them and so they left as soon as the wagons were packed with supplies and tents.

In mid-July 1861, Grants regiment crossed the Mississippi, as soon as they reached shores in northeastern Missouri; they supported other troops against the enemy of Southern fighters.

On 18 August, Grant took off for St. Louis; he was in St. Louis on 19 August and in Jefferson City on 21 August where his next command was. In Jefferson City, there were many Union troops, but Grant did not see them as soldiers. All in all Jefferson City was a complete madhouse.

Grant reached Cairo on 4th of September in order to establish the command post for the district of southeast Missouri that he was best qualified for. It would be the key command in the west.

When Grant walked into the town unnoticed and into a bank; that had been converted into Army Headquarters, he was now in command of troops in Southern Mississippi and also in charge of warships.

On 6 September, Grant with the Union troops took Paducah, Kentucky. The following 7th of November, Grant suffers a tactical defeat at Belmont, Mo.

In 1862, the 6th day of February, Grant and Flag Officer Andrew Foote lead a successful joint army attack upon Fort Henry on the Tennessee River.

16 February 1862, Brig. Gen. Simon B. Buckner unconditionally surrenders 15,000 captured confederates to Grant. While other confederates abandon Nashville, Tenn.

17 March 1862 Grant assumes command of the Federal Army at Pittsburg Landing, Tennessee.

On 6 April a surprise attack at Shiloh, Tenn., (Pittsburg Landing) the confederates maul Grants army, also fatally wounding A. S. Johnson, and Beauregard takes command of the Rebel army.

Once again, Buell's reinforcements helping Grant at Shiloh turns the battle in the Federals favor, forcing Beauregard to retreat to Corinth, Miss.

By February 1863, Grant cuts the levee at Yazoo Pass, Mississippi, to open passage for gunboats to reach the rear of Vicksburg by way of the Yazoo River. Following Grants Yazoo Pass expedition blocked Fort Pemberton.

Then on 30 April, Grant with his forces crosses the Mississippi River to Bruinsburg, Miss., South of Vicksburg. 1 May his regiment defeats the confederates at Port Gibson, Miss.

After Grants several assaults on Vicksburg the city fails. Then when McClernard insisted that he was close to a breakthrough on his front, Grant ordered renewal of the assault, but the only result was an increase of casualties.

Commanding Officer Grant believing at last that a siege was necessary for the Union not to be defeated, Grant ordered his troops to implanting batteries and digging trenches around the city.

The siege began and after constant shelling and the Union troops closing in on the city, when Pemberton's army was at a breaking point; Pemberton sent a white flag through the lines and asked for terms. Grant followed with his unconditional surrender line, but receded from it quickly when Pemberton refused to go for it; and then on 4 July Pemberton surrendered the city and the army, on terms, which permitted his men to give their paroles and go to their homes.

Late in September 1863, it was discovered the whole Union army was trapped in Chattanooga, low on rations and in danger of capture by the Confederate army.

Realizing the situation the command was given to Officer Grant of the West, and things started getting better. Sherman brought troops in from Memphis to help and two more groups moved in from the Army in the Potomac.

The Union troops on foot traveling down Lookout Mountain heading for the Western and Atlantic Railroad, that ran through Chattanooga to Atlanta, which was Braggs supply line. As the Union troops entered Chattanooga, Bragg's troops had to evacuate.

The end of November the fighting came to a halt after continuous charging from the Yankees, and Grant became commander of the whole Union Army and Sherman took command in the West.

In the spring, Chattanooga became the jump off point for the invasion of South's mid-land. During the night 7-8 May the two armies made their way down dark roads in the exhausting race for a tiny settlement called Spotsylvania Court House. Lee's army of N. Virginia gets there first. After several days of fighting Lee's confederates form a semicircle covering Spotsylvania attacking with Hammocks II Corps massed on a narrow front.

Then Grant succeeded in making a hole in the center of the Rebel line, capturing guns and men. After about four and one half hours of continuous fighting, Lee puts together a new defensive line across the base of the Salient and assembles his forces behind it, ending the action.

Early dawn on 12 May, Grant sent Hancock's men out attacking on Mule Shoe Salient, at the center of Lee's lines the defenders were overrun and confiscated twenty guns and thousands of prisoners, including two generals and most of the Stonewall brigade.

The confederates counter-attack knocked them back to the first line of trenches. The Union troops held there, regrouped and what followed was a struggle determining to be the end.

The Northerners were piled up thirty-deep, due to the narrow front. At the end bends in the lines was hand-to-hand fighting with unbelievable blood-thirst, cannons fired at close range and soldiers were stabbed to death with bayonets.

The bloodshed continued in the rain and smoky-dusk and dim of night, well past mid-night, ending when Lee completed a new line across the Salient.

As the Civil War neared its end, in February 1865 Sherman and his forces headed toward North Carolina where he would connect with Schofield and his 21,000 troops.

The Rebels, in order to halt Sherman, Joe Johnson was pulled out of retirement and put in charge of about 30,000 confederate troops that had been pulled out of Savanna. Johnston being pulled out of retirement was a sign that the defense of the Southern states army was dwelling.

Sherman's men had special qualities, men who had lived close to the frontier, backwoodsmen who could use an axe who could move their ways through almost any obstacle as they traveled north through Savannah, Georgia, then to South Carolina.

As Sherman's army continued moving south, they sliced through the railroad lines that led to Charleston and the city fell to the Union.

At Fort Sumter, the national flag went up on the rubble-heap, as General Sherman's troops marched on into North Carolina. When they reached N. Carolina, they felt no need to do any destruction for they felt that soon the war would end.

The situation with Grants Union troops against Lee's Confederates was still going on. General Lee was faced with double numbers while heading toward North Carolina, hoping that he could slip through Grants lines, get to North Carolina and hook-up with Johnsons regiment and beat Sherman and then turn back and meet Grant on terms. The battle between Grants army and Lee's army continued until one of Lee's men came forward with a white flag in a sign of surrender.

Grant retired from the military during the year 1869. In addition, accepted the Presidency of the United States 4 March 1869, and served until 4 March 1877. Ulysses S. Grant at the age of 63 years passed away 23 July 1885.

1890-Battle of Wounded Knee

Mass grave for the dead Indians after the massacre
December 29, 1890, the U.S. Cavalry troops went into the camp to disarm the Sioux Indians at Wounded Knee Creek of the Pine Ridge Indian Reservation in South Dakota. One version of events claims that during the process of disarming the Indians, a deaf tribesman named Black was reluctant to give up his rifle, claiming he had paid a lot for it. Simultaneously, an old man was performing a ritual called the Ghost Dance. Black's rifle went off at that point, and the U.S. Army began shooting at the Native Americans. The disarmed Indian warriors did their best to fight back. By the time the massacre was over, between 250 and 300 men, women, and children of the Sioux Indians had been killed and 51 were wounded (4 men and 47 women and children, some of whom died later); some estimates placed the number of dead at 300. Twenty-five soldiers also died, and 39 were wounded (six of the wounded later died). At least twenty soldiers were awarded the Medal of Honor. In 2001, the National Congress of American Indians passed two resolutions condemning the military awards and called on the U.S. government to rescind them.

CHAPTER SIX

WORLD WAR ONE

World War One- 1914-1919...Triple Alliance: Germany, Italy, and Austria-Hungary vs. Triple Entente: Britain, France, and Russia.

The United States joined on the side of the Triple Entente (treaty) in 1917.

It is well known in the American History books that long before the Americans entered into that war, that the German-Foreign Minister, while his country was at peace with the United States, had urged the German Minister in Mexico to arrange for a Mexican Invasion of the United States promising to Mexico a slice of the American territory.

At the time, when in 1914 the Americas' were doing very well with its democratic independence, a system promoting the interest of the people. It had been at peace since the Civil War had ended. The country itself was young, only century and a half years old. While on the other side of the world Germany and other European countries were many centuries old.

The United States was not looking for war, they were content to stay neutral until after the Germans sunk the Lusitania, murdered Nurse Cavell and converted Northern France into a wilderness of death and destruction; the American people started to take notice. Officially, during that time, United States still neutral, and the United States President Woodrow Wilson had sent several exchanges of notes to Germany, the last one closed with a declaration that if Germany violated the rights of the U.S. upon the high seas, the United States, would hold her at "strict accountability".

Following President Wilson's last note, the last day of January 1917, Germany announced to the world that she would wage war on the sea with unrestricted frightfulness. Thus, she repudiated her pledges to the U.S., and intimated that she would torpedo without warning every ship that dared to sail the seas.

On 2 April 1917, President Wilson went before congress and asked that diplomatic relations with Germany be severed; his last hope that the United States would be able to maintain armed neutrality, soon vanished.

The Senate passed the war declaration on 4 April by a vote of 82 to 6, and the House of Representatives passed the vote on 6 April by 373 to 50 votes. Twenty-two days after the declaration of war, Congress passed conscription of our law providing for the selective draft.

In a few weeks the regular Army, by volunteering the count grew to the strength of 287,000 troops and the National Guard up to 625,000 troops. On 5 June, ten million young Americans registered and became available, when required for the purposes of national cause.

The Allies also made the most urgent representations of the U.S. to speed up the transportation of troops in Europe. Although the United States was preparing for war during 1919-1920, they were far behind in providing airplanes, guns and munitions.

The American Army was without adequate divisional organization and full equipment for the troops when they landed in France for training. The Allies, however, persuaded the U.S. to rush forward troops promising to make up all deficiencies, themselves.

General Pershing was appointed the Chief Command of the United States Expeditionary Forces, and the first contingent of trained American troops submitted to be brigaded for service with British and French troops would go forward at the rate of 250,000 a month.

From then on there was no stopping the American Soldier, the United States men fought alone and with the Allies; the British, French, Italians, Russians, Belgians, Serbians and the Romanians. They fought at Chateau-Thierry, St. Mihiel, the Argonne Forest, the Mossell River, Metz, the Woevie Forest, Port-surf-seille, etc. It was a horrific price paid in blood, tears and money to save our civilization and freedom. Following is another gallant single military veteran that was among those 250,000 troops.

Kraft, Howard R. 129th Field Artillery, Battery "C"

England, France, Germany 05/29/1918-05/03/1919

Donated to me by Jean Lamping, wife of Veteran William Lamping featured in my third book; she offered me her stepfather's military history now documented in the Liberty of Congress and always is available for family and friends.

A World War One Veteran, Tells about his time spent while a Soldier in 129th Field Artillery, Battery "C": Howard R. Kraft, was born 17 June 1897, in Waukegan, Illinois, Cook County, he enlisted in the US Army during World War 1, on 29 May 1918, before his 21st birthday. After his basic training at Jefferson Barracks, MO, Howard was assigned to Battery "C", 129th Field Artillery, 35th Division.

Battery "C" organized at Independence, Mo., shortly after the declaration of war by our Country upon Germany, "Battery C" mustered into the Federal Service in that City on Sunday, 5 August 1917.

At that time, Battery "C" consisted of one Captain, 2 LT's and two second LT's, and had one hundred and thirty-six enlisted men.

Following is a little story that I would like to share with my readers, it is all about the true journey that the Veterans of Battery "C" experienced upon the call to duty way back when the United States Senate passed the vote in April 1917, to join the allies in the Battle of World War One.

Independence, Missouri the home of a large majority of the eligible men for military service was in gala attire. The Courthouse lawn and square immediately began to assume the appearance of real war times with guns and soldiers; the Armory being the quarters of the boys, was the scene of many brilliant occasions.

The order of the day was foot and drill exercise, and anxiously watched by the admiring sweethearts, wives, mothers, fathers and friends until the evening of 26 September 1917.

When orders came to move, the entire population of the city turned out en-masse to give the boys a rousing send-off as they marched to the awaiting train on their first lap of a long journey to the shell swept battlefields of France.

After two days travel through the states of Kansas and Oklahoma, they arrived at Camp Doniphan or Fort Still, Oklahoma in early morning. After a march to camp, tents pitched and army life had become a reality.

Shortly after arrival, three Captains took command of the Battery. On 10 November 1917, work and drill kept all of the men busy and time did not hang very heavily. The Battalion's first war lesson began with the construction of modern battle trenches and gun emplacements near Signal Mountain.

About a month later on 24 January 1918, a banquet and get-together meeting took place at the Battery. Many distinguished visitors were present, among them Brigadier General Berry (and his aide Major Gale), LT. Col. Robert M. Danford, Majors Miles, Stayton and Wilson and Capt. Sermon. The officers gave interesting speeches full of advice, encouragement and suggestions that were highly appreciated and well received. The music for the occasion was furnished by the women of the Lawton Music Club.

Intensive training of mounted drills, regardless of the weather conditions, was scheduled for the Battery until 8 May 1918, when orders to prepare to move were received, and on 10 May entrained for Camp Mills, NY via the Frisco. Their first stop was Oklahoma City, OK. Then on to Springfield, Missouri for a short stop.

After a day's riding they arrived in Pacific, Missouri, where they left the train for a short hike, then on to St. Louis arriving there about 6:00 P.M. About 9:00 P.M., they entrained in modern Pullmans, on the clover Leaf, and the next stop was Frankfort, Indiana and passing through Toledo and Cleveland, Ohio and Buffalo, New York. In Buffalo, the Red Cross served refreshments to the troops.

At Hoboken, New Jersey, the soldiers transferred to a ferry for Long Island and arrived at Camp Mills, 14 May 1918.

On 20 May, they received sailing orders, marched to the Canard piers, and embarked about 10:00 A.M. on the Saxonia (R.M.S.) and at 5:00 P.M. they began their long trip to France. On 23 May, the troops anchored off Halifax, N.S. and had a good view of the ruins of that city caused by the recent explosion of war munitions, probably the worst of its kind during the war.

After 17 days on the ocean, the American troops anchored at Tilbury Docks, London, England, on the night of 4 June 1918, and disembarked on the morning of 5 June 1918. They immediately entrained for Winchester, England, then to Southampton where they embarked for La Havre, France on the steamship Viper, one of the swiftest ships in the British service.

Here the real tension of the trip began to be realized; especially by the officers. The English Channel, through which they were passing, had been the scene of disaster to many troop ships. Floating mines of the enemy, together with her many recent submarine activities, had wrought havoc to many British ships.

They arrived safely at La Havre on the morning of 8 June 1918, where they remained for a couple of days, fraternizing with the "Tommie's," and on the night of 10 June entrained for Angers, France, arriving there on the 11th and then a short "hike" brought them to the ancient French village of Andard.

It was at Andard that they received their famous "French Seventy-fives", together with some horses. Being the first American troops in that section of France, they were accorded a royal welcome by the entire populace.

On 16 June 1918, the entire regiment marched to Brain, Regimental Chaplain; Father Curtis L. Tierman blessed the colors in a large Cathedral.

On 17 August 1918, they broke camp and marched to Guer, entrained for Saulzures, where they arrived on 20 August and after a three day rest they began their march into German Territory. "The historical Alsace-Lorraine country", crossing the Vosges Mountains, at the extreme summit of which is a large stone marker, erected by Germany designating the dividing line between France and Alsace-Lorraine; they arrived at Kruth, situated in a valley, between two mountains, on 24 August 1918. It being a strong pro-German town in Germany territory, their reception was not a very cordial one.

The batteries arrived Sunday morning about 4:30 and they immediately went into position, and prepared to go into action, but none too soon. The Germans began a terrified bombardment of gas, shrapnel and high explosives about nightfall, but they gave them shell for shell throughout the night, and with dawn the firing ceased. This was now near the town of Mettach.

Immediately across the valley was a splendid view of Robinson Hill, made famous by the stand of the Alpine Chasseurs, better known as the "Blue Devils of France," in the latter part of 1914 and up to the "Battle of Meterzal" on 15 June 1915. Here the <u>French lost about 60,000 men.</u>

On the evening of 6 September 1918, they marched to the village of Cloyvilliers, there they were billeted in barns and remained there until

9 September, then started northward, and after a long, tiresome march, bivouacked in the early morning hours in woods near Nancy.

The rain came down in torrents and mud was shoe to mouth deep. After trudging many weary kilometers, they passed through the city of Nancy about 2:00 A.M. The city of Nancy is one of the largest and best-known cities of France, presenting a weird scene while they marched through its streets; where not a light was shown and no one except a lone sentry in sight.

After leaving Nancy, at a high ridge road, they witnessed one of the greatest artillery duels the world has ever known; the horizon was lighted up as though it were an electrical display. It was the great St. Muriel drive. The Company moved into the Forest De Haye, directly in the rear of St. Mihiel, the troops waited in reserve with horse's harnessed and full equipment on carriages, ready at any minute to advance and take position in line should they be needed.

They again took up the march on 15 September 1918. This proved to be the longest and hardest of any of the hikes yet experienced.

The horses were dying from exhaustion and exposure; feed was scarce and the roads heavy. Carcasses of dead horses lined the roadside. The men carrying full packs were footsore, weary, and virtually living on iron rations, still with some words of cheer from our officers they kept on without a murmur, and finally arrived in another forest where they rested for two days and a night.

After more traveling on 21 September, they halted in a shell torn field. In the afternoon, they had moved about a kilometer forward and established battery array in a draw. They remained until after the greatest American battle ever fought, "The Battle of Argonne Forest."

About noon, 21 September 1918, orders were to have the firing batteries in readiness to move forward at any time, and about 5:00 P.M. they pulled out, to take up their position on Hill 290.

They proceeded up a shell swept, camouflaged road, past their ammunition dump, in rain, mud and darkness. Here, they left the road and took out across a field with virtually no road and mud hub deep, the horses in bad shape, they arrived at their positions.

It was here that they experienced their first German barrage. In addition, the Germans were gassing heavily. The morning of 26 September, was to begin the great offensive along the entire front. Battery "C" was selected to accompany the infantry in their advance.

This was the greatest drive ever launched against the Hun and later proved his "Waterloo". Throughout the night of the 25th, and into the morning of the 26th the Hun kept pounding at them with guns of all calibers. At 1:00 A.M. of the 26th, the Allies began the great drive.

In a distance, the horizon had the appearance of a severe electrical storm. Their guns were in action everywhere, the land is rolling here and it seemed as though the very hills opened up and commenced to belch fire and flame.

They kept a continuous barrage from 4:20 A.M. to 7:20 A.M. firing approximately 2,500 rounds of ammunition for the one battery. After the guns of the enemy were silenced, the troops pulled their guns, and prepared to advance to support their infantry who had already gone "over the top"; they were now in Boureuilles where the blowing up of bridges by the retreating enemy stopped their advance. Ahead to the left front, they could see their infantry desperately charging up a slope and attacking the machine gun pits of the enemy. The German airplanes were trying to harass them, but Allied planes were directly overhead.

On 27 September in a heavy rain they advanced to the woods and went into position northeast of Hill 239, moving again at 6 A.M. they went into position about 400 meters southeast of Hill 221, where they fired several barrages on Carpentry and Baulny. Here they remained throughout the night.

Early on the morning of the 28th, they received orders to move to Charpentry to cover their advance.

Advancing they passed through Cheppy and on to Charpentry. Enroute they met captured batteries of German 77's, German machine gun nests with their own men piled high in front of them; men dead and dying lined the roadside, mutilated horses, destroyed guns, and material of all kinds, presented a scene that is impossible to describe.

They were now on the Route Nationate, here their advance was continually meeting stiff resistance by attacks from the enemy airplanes that would sweep down parallel with their column and turn loose volley after volley of machine gun fire. Here they suffered their first casualty in the death of Private Robert K. Mayfield. A shell passed through one of their garrisons, instantly killing Mayfield on the opposite side.

They were now moving into Charpentry; crossing a bridge spanning the Aisne River, they took cover in an old orchard near the ruins of this village, laid their guns and immediately went into action.

The German trenches and dugouts here showed why they had held this line for four years.

They found the enemy trenches fortified with rock walls and their dugouts were in many instances 40 feet below the ground, with all the conveniences of home, electric lights, baths, kitchen, dining room and sleeping quarters.

Some of their U. S. troops who had been on short rations for the past few days, in exploring the hastily abandoned quarters, found jam, molasses, butter and course black bread, also some Belgian hares, which were doubtless being raised for the Hun officer's; contributed to the feast and enjoyed by them.

Allied tanks began streaming past us, coming from the front; then a squadron of cavalry was seen falling back; stragglers of the infantry passed and informed them that the Germans had broken the line and were coming over (which report proved to be incorrect) however, the Hun made three counterattacks all of which were repulsed.

After being relieved by the First Division on 4 October they retired to Signeulles, about 40 kilometers in the rear, for a few days of much needed rest. Arriving at Signeulles, many men were unfit for immediate service and were left at field hospitals to recuperate while the remaining part of the battery took up the march again.

On 12 October, they left Signeulles, still raining as usual, and after an all night hike spent the day in a forest. In Rapt they spent a day, they were now moving into the Woevre sector of the world's famous Verdun front. The fighting in this sector had been dilatory for the past two years, the French having established their lines with the aid of their many forts.

The enemy having been aroused by the activities along the entire line was preparing for a big drive in the sector also, as the divisions of the Yanks began to pour in. They arrived in the forest near Ft. Rozellier, in the morning of 16 October.

On 9 November, orders were to advance and support the 81st Division Infantry who were going over the top. At 11:00 A.M. they moved forward, Battery "C" of the First Battalion, and Batteries E and F of the Second Battalion. Arriving in position near Moulainville De Bosse, they were in an open field, looking across a marsh with a dense growth of underbrush, probably four feet high.

Their guns were laid in waiting on the early morning of the 10th, all this being done in darkness and the usual rain. The rain continued throughout the entire day, gradually getting worse as the day wore on. The heavy weather had prevented the enemy from getting range on them, although they kept up continual firing throughout the day and night. This weather continued throughout the morning of the 11th. At 9:00 A.M. they received orders to cease firing at 11:00 A.M. and were being advised of the signing of the armistice.

However, they continued to fire until about 10:30 A.M. when the weather began to clear, the fog lifted and the enemy was starting to locate them with their large caliber guns. Shells began breaking all around with several hitting close shattering a wheel. All this time the enemy had been throwing a sweeping barrage.

At 11:00 A.M. the firing eased almost as suddenly as it had begun over four years before. A deep silence seemed to fall over the entire line. There were no wild demonstrations; no cheers; the seriousness of the war had been impressed too firmly upon the minds of the men to be thrown off in a few minutes.

To Howard Kraft and the men in gun pits, with pieces ready for action and plenty of ammunition and the fighting spirit at "high tide", it was hard to realize that the last mission had been performed. By noon, the clouds had broken away. The sun began to shine for the first time in weeks. The afternoon was bright and crisp.

That night, the moon shone out in its entire splendor. "No Man's Land" that night was basking in the mellow moonlight instead of the flashings of the cannons that had held sway so long. A sight will long remain in the minds of all who gazed across that expanse of country dividing the two lines that memorable night of 11 November 1918.

On the morning of the 12th, they were ordered to return to original positions; remaining here for a few days, then pulled their guns and returned to the echelon about two kilometers distant in the woods and hills, at Camp Claire Cote. Here time was taken up in the regular routine of fatigues and drills. Time soon began to hang heavily on their hands as the days wore on.

They were located in an isolated place, with nothing to divert our minds; no amusements of any sort; expecting any day to leave for somewhere (either Germany or home, but preferably home) and believing almost any rumor, but holding firmly to the ones which favored early return home.

Arriving at Camp Claire Cote, they found the billets, stables and surroundings in a deplorable condition. The billets were put in good shape; the stables were reconstructed and put in good condition; kitchen was enlarged and improved; and an old stable was thoroughly renovated.

On 21 January 1919, they began hiking out of the woods and hills, away from the shell-swept, battle-scarred fields of Northern France and after two days arrived at the small ancient French village of Culey.

Howard H. Kraft received his honorable discharge from the Army, 3 May 1919 at Great Camp, Illinois. For his military service, he had earned several medals and ribbons.

World War 1 casualties suffered by the participants dwarfed those of previous wars: some 8,500,000 soldiers died because of wounds and/or disease. The greatest number of casualties and wounds were inflicted by artillery, followed by small arms, and then by poison gas. The bayonet that was relied on by the prewar French Army as the decisive weapon actually produced few casualties.

On even a quiet day on the Western Front, many hundreds of Allied and German soldiers died. The heaviest loss of life for a single day occurred on the first day of July 1916, during the Battle of the Somme, when the British Army suffered 57,470 casualties.

Sir Winston Churchill once described the battles of the Somme and Verdun, which were typical of trench warfare in their futile and indiscriminate slaughter, as being waged between double or triple walls of cannons fed by mountains of shells. In an open space surrounded by masses of these guns large numbers of infantry divisions collided.

They fought in this dangerous position until battered into a state of uselessness. Then other divisions replaced them. So many men were lost in the process and shattered beyond recognition that there is a French monument at Verdun to the 150,000 un-located dead that are presumed to be buried in the vicinity.

At the end of World War One there was a parade in New York City, on Fifth Avenue. It happened on a very cold day in February. There had never been a parade on Fifth Avenue with such an out-pouring of citizens to welcome home its Soldiers of the 369th Regiment, on 17 February 1919.

The Harlem Hellfighters had come home from the war. The black people came in taxis; they came in cars, some in horse drawn carriages. The women were bundled in shawls or blankets against the cold winter air. They were brimming brightly as the whole stand applauded. Today was their day and they were proud to be part of it.

When Governor Smith arrived along with other city officials, the crowd greeted them with a hit song by Irving Berlin. At that moment the parade arriving with the foremost in position were four platoons of mounted police riding their horses twelve abreast.

Next in line was Colonel William Hayward, the Colonel had trained and drilled them back in 1913. He was followed by the Police Department Band, and finally came the guest of honor, the 369th, infantry; they were almost three thousand strong marching twenty abreast in tight formation, an action they were taught by the French soldiers who had been their brothers in battle.

By the time the parade reached 60th Street, the crowd estimated at about 250,000. The parade of troops were marching so quickly that they only had time to smile as they marched past their wives and children

Following the parade of soldiers was a fleet of ambulances with nearly two-hundred Hellfighters that were too wounded to march. With its band playing military marches and the soldiers marching in formation, every living sole watched, every fire escape, every rooftop, every window, and every sidewalk along the parade route was jam-packed.

After the parade ended, the soldiers were awarded with a dinner reception at the 71st, Regiment Armory. Inside the Armory were more than 3,000 Harlemites in the galleries. It became so packed that the soldiers had to eat standing up.

The day ended with the soldiers taking a train to Camp Upton, on Long Island, on the following day they were discharged and became civilians again.

History has it that no other American soldiers saw harder or more constant fighting and none gave a better account of themselves, whether in the Chamagne, at Chateau Thierry, at the Saint Mihiel salient or in the Argonne. When fighting was needed to be done, the Harlem fighters were there to serve.

Similar uncertainties exist about the number of civilian deaths attributable to the war. There were no agencies established to keep records of these fatalities, but it is clear that the displacement of peoples through the movement of the war in Europe and in Asia Minor, accompanied as it was in 1918 by the most destructive outbreak of influenza in history, led to the deaths of large numbers. It is estimated the number of civilian deaths attributable to the war was higher than the military casualties, or around 13,000,000. Causes of civilian deaths had been largely due to <u>starvation</u>, exposure, disease, military encounters, and massacres.

World War I had ended: A salute for the winners is in order, and the Allied leaders quickly gathered in Paris for making treaties. The treaties were signed in Paris suburbs. The vocabulary the delegates used to write the treaties were negligent of factuality, (which unfortunately lead them into another war) instead it spoke of hope. Among the delegates was President Woodrow Wilson of the United States. Back home the U. S. Senate repulsed the Versailles Treaty and the League of Nations.

During 1922, staff officers in Germany's homeland arranged with manufactures to produce high volumes of military equipment such as aircraft, tanks, rifles, machine guns and other armor, as they were preparing for a secret war. Russia was manufacturing dive-bombers, and other metal aircraft long before other countries had blueprints for the design of them.

Adolf Hitler in his early young adult years was unknown. He was Austrian born, an unsuccessful young man that lived in a home for vagabonds, in the slum district of Vienna, doing odd jobs and unwanted paintings. His only interest in life was politics he had no other interest in life.

Hitler's career in World War One, earned him the Silver Cross. After the war, he became involved in plots that fermented inside Germany such as the beer hall 1923 Putsch in Munich. Hitler was tried and convicted and was imprisoned in Landsberg Prison for nine months. Hitler's famous book "Mein Kampf" that he wrote while in prison sold well to some of the Germans that believed it and became followers, very few foreigners cared for it.

In Hitler's publication of Mein Kampf he publishes a cynical delight in his attacks on the treaty and it wasn't long after that he realizes his impact on the citizens because they too were depressed that Germany had lost the war that Germany started, and many citizens were looking for a leader, a public advocate, to lead them and get vengeance; at his meetings he used the same approach by addressing the Versailles terms.

In addition, in 1933 Hitler was in control of a political party that he and his followers created called the National Socialist (Nazi) Party. An election held and only about one out of every three voted for the party, yet Hitler gained control of the Reichstag. During the next six years until 1939 and World War II broke out Hitler became dictator and Germany a strong military power; he had started secretly in 1921 putting the unemployed and the discontented into uniforms. Democracy vanished; he liquidated the Jewish population, and stamped out party dissidents through terror or sometimes-outright murder.

In the United States, Wall Street's gaping failure started at the end of 1929, for a decade, America falsely believed that it was the leading power in economics. Then on 24 October 1929, Americans started to shiver, and by end of October, the worst financial days in American history happened when almost thirteen million shares were unloaded. Investors had lost thirty million dollars. By 1933 twelve million were unemployed, mortgages were foreclosed and mines and factories shutdown.

In 1933, Roosevelt arrived in Washington, and came with the promise of relief. In his first hundred days in office, Roosevelt was able to establish a new style and direction in Federal Government that would do more to change life in America than any other Administration. By the time Hitler succeeded in fueling another war, the U. S. was again on its feet.

Mussolini was on the scene in December of 1934, anxious to show the world his Fascist troops and expand his new Roman Empire in Africa; he provoked a border skirmish at Walwal, on the border of Ethiopia. Although, the Emperor appealed for help to the League of Nations, the League did nothing because the Great Powers refused to intervene.

In America during the roaring twenties, the things remembered for were prohibition, speakeasies, and home brew. It was a decade of jazz and the Charleston. Al Capone and rival gangster mobs whom machined-gunned each other over bootleg business. It was a time of million dollar boxing gates, home run kings and sports mania.

<u>It was the time that Brig. Gen. William Mitchell cried about the importance of building air power and "no one listened"</u>!

CHAPTER SEVEN

WORLD WAR TWO

Wholesale Murder of Lidice, Czechoslovakia: In March of 1938 Czechoslovakia vanished, when Adolf Hitler occupied the rest of Czech lands. The remaining part of Slovakia became a Nazi puppet state.

In order to suppress anti-fascist resistance movement, security police chief, SS Reinhard Heydrich was appointed Deputy Reich's-protector in 1941. To his accomplishment five-thousand anti-fascist were imprisoned. On 27 May 1942 Heydrich was assassinated by two Czech patriots.

When Hitler learned of the assassination of Heydrich, mass executions of the Czech took place. In June 1942, one-hundred-seventy-three males were executed, plus about thirteen other males that had come back to the village were killed. The one-hundred and eighty-four women and eighty-eight children were deported to concentration camps; a few children were considered suitable for Germanization and handed over to SS families; the rest were sent to the Chelmno extermination camp where they were gassed. After the war only one-hundred-fifty-three women and seventeen children returned. Hitler wanted the town wiped off the map, he ordered his troops to remove all visible remains of the village, re-route the stream running through it and the roads in and out. Then they covered the village with dirt and planted trees.

The information of what happened to Lidice was found out by the Allied armies and in September 1942 coal miners in Stoke-on-Trent, Staffordshire, in Great Britain led by a doctor by the name of Barnett Stross, who in 1945 became a local MP, founded the organization

"Lidice Shall Live" to raise funds for the rebuilding of the village after the war.

After the Second World War women from Lidice who survived imprisonment at Ravensbruck, returned and were rehoused in the new village of Lidice that was built overlooking the original site.

A sculpture from the 1990s by Marie Uchytilova, overlooks the site of the old village of Lidice. Entitled "The Memorial to the Children Victims of the War", it comprises eighty – three bronze statues of children (43 girls and 40 boys) aged 1 to 16, to honor the children who were murdered at Chelmno in the summer of 1942.

In 1939 both Hitler and Stalin wanted war. On 1 September at 4:45 A.M. the Germans attacked Poland. On 3 September Britain and France delivered a warning to Germany, to withdraw the military forces from Poland by mid-night. However, when no reply was received, both countries affirmed war on Germany.

Although the Pope, President Roosevelt, and the King of Belgium appealed for peace, fifty-six German divisions, nine armored, rolled toward Warsaw, Bialystok, Cracow, and Lvov, in Poland and on its boarder. In addition, fifteen hundred Luftwaffe planes, including divebombers smashed the Polish towns and villages. The Poles were ruined. A Polish state no longer exists. Germany took 71,000 square miles, Russia about 75,000 square miles. Russia suffered almost no loss, while Germany admitted 10, 572 killed and claimed 450,000 prisoners.

After his winning of Poland, Hitler turned his sight on Finland, with the support of Russian troops they decided to subdue Finland. November 1939, the Soviet planes bombed Helsinki and other Finland cities. In addition, the Red Army rolled across Finland's boarder at five different points. The League of Nation responded by expelling the Soviet Union in December 1939. In March 1940, Finland signed a peace treaty with the Soviets.

After Finland, the warriors shifted their attention to the Scandinavians and Sweden's iron mines. With British strategic interest beginning to focus on Germans industrial dependence on Swedish iron, they studied ways of blocking this route. Although the British Royal Navy was able to land a considerable army around Narvik, Norway the Royal Air Force was based too far away to provide the desperately needed cover and the allied troops were pinned against the sea and eventually routed when Hitler overwhelmed France.

Hitler's troops went on and succeeded in sealing off Europe's northern flank, insuring access to Sweden's iron, and closing off the Baltic. From late summer 1939, until late spring 1940, the British with all its ocean power showed very little overseas land expeditions and only able to supply limited air coverage. The French, waited for the inevitable. United States President Roosevelt sought to intervene, but didn't.

On 10 May Winston Churchill became Britain's Prime Minister. That same day Hitler began its surge against Holland, Belgium, and Luxembourg.

The Germans had a plan to defeat France, it was named Case Yellow. The plan called for an armored trust through the Ardennes, past Sedan to the Channel. It consisted of tanks, followed by motorized infantry and Stuka dive-bombers plus paratroopers that landed behind allied lines.

A force of about one-hundred-seventeen divisions took part in the attack. At Fort Eben Emael, the most vital of the strongholds, some twelve hundred Belgian defenders capitulated to only eighty Germans. In addition, on 28 May 1940, Belgians King Leopold II surrendered the Belgian Army unconditionally. The Belgium surrender exposed the entire left flank of the Anglo-French defenses, and France itself was crumbling fast.

German tanks proceeded to drive the allied forces north toward the channel, cut them off and the forces retreated to the Port of Dunkirk where approximately a third of a million men that were trapped at the port until a brigade of boats from England rescued them. The story of the rescue is horrific and written in many history books.

The Germans continued pushing, regrouping and fighting for the battle of France, by 14 June 1940 they occupied Paris. The French army was dwindling, thousands of refugees were heading south to escape the Nazi Army; some people in cars, some on foot pulling wagons, or pushing wheel-barrows containing a small content of survival items. The hospitals had been evacuated earlier; patients were taken to other places where they could be safe.

During the evacuation, the refugees had to jump down in ditches in order to dodge the overhead Nazi flyers that were dropping their bombs on them. While hugging the ground the people could hear groaning that perhaps people had been hit, but no one would leave the ground in fear that they would be next.

Etta Shiber was one of those evacuees that I read about in a gripping evacuating documentary from a book written by her that featured her and her friend Kitty, two young women that were refugees trying to escape Paris and captured by the Nazis and held prisoners. In May of 1942, Etta, being a United States citizen, was released in exchange for a German prisoner that was being held in the United States, by the name of Johanna Hoffmann; Johanna was convicted of being a Nazi spy. The name of the book is titled "Paris Underground".

Next, the Germans capture the Channel Islands and the Battle of Britain begins with Nazi flyers over England's southern coast wiping-out port facilities. July 1940, the "Battle of the Atlantic" becomes intense as convoys duel with U-boats. President Roosevelt calls for a bill signing for four billion dollars for two hundred vessels including seven battleships and a two ocean-navy.

By September 1940, Nazi flyers open blitz on London, London evacuates children to other countries like America and Switzerland, etc... The attack continues until the flyers are restrained by bad weather.

On 16 September, United States adopted a Selective Service of men between ages 21 to 26 that are required to register for military training, by October; over sixteen million American men registered under Selective Service. At the end of September, a United States Marine detachment landed on Midway Island to organize new defenses.

The end of December 1940, United States office of production expedites shipments of material aid to Britain, and on 9 April 1941 U. S. undertakes defense of Greenland so it can set up a military base there.

Once again, in early May the Luftwaffe deluges London with bombs, starting thousands of fires and badly damaging hundreds of buildings among them is the House of Commons. (Ref. Amer. Heritage WWII Chronology)

Hitler's deputy Rudolf Hess secretly parachutes to Scotland to bring a private peace plan to make Germany and Britain allies against Bolshevism (a Russian movement founded by Vladimir Lenin), Prime Minister Churchill has him imprisoned. Hitler disowns him.

On 21 May, a German U-boat sinks the American merchant ship, the Robin Moor off Brazil. Then on 16 of June, the U. S. closes the German consular offices and orders Hitler's officials to leave the country. In addition, on 7 July 1941 United States forces land in Iceland to relieve British troops there.

Also in July of 1941, an experiment was going on at the Tuskegee Institute in Alabama by the Army Air Corp, testing African-American pilots to see if they could fly. It all began when First Lady, Eleanor Roosevelt accepted a ride from an African-American pilot in 1940, James Barbour, a Tuskegee Airman who flew with the Class 45G during World War Two.

When she returned to Washington, the first lady wondered why the military wasn't accepting African-American pilot, Barbour said. In response the Army Air Corp established the experiment in Alabama.

The experiment which started in July 1941 proved that they could fly, and so the African-American pilots were assigned as the Tuskegee Airmen serving as bomber escorts, and had the achievement of never losing a single bomber to the enemy fire. They were also the first African-American military pilots.

By the middle of October things started getting more hostile when a German U-boat damages United States destroyer "Kearny" off Iceland, and U-562 torpedoes sink United States destroyer "Reuben James, off Iceland, with a loss of 115 Americans.

In the summer of 1940 polls indicated that a majority of Americans did not want the country involved in Europe's wars. Although, President Franklin D. Roosevelt's military and State Department leaders agreed that Nazi Germany would threaten the national security of the United States. They felt that Americans needed a call to action.

Written by Lieutenant Commander Arthur H. McCollum, a five-page memorandum was given to FDR's two trusted advisors. The memorandum drafted October 1940, called for a plan that would provoke Japan into an overt act of war against the United States. The plan put forward an outline to maneuver an opening that would give United States a motive into joining the axis against the German forces. Although according to most history books, the United States history documentation about what led up to the bombing of Pearl Harbor is written differently.

So the real question remains, did FDR, use the memorandum as a guideline and provoke the attack? Were there earlier covert moves by the United States? According to a secret strategy memo, dated 7 October 1940, and adopted by the President, there were.

To learn more about the five page memo outlining the maneuvers that did take place leading up to the attack on America, can be found in a book written in detail by Robert B. Stinnett, the titled is, "Day of Deceit".

CHAPTER EIGHT

BOMBING OF PEARL HARBOR

On 7 December 1941, the Japanese struck with treachery characteristic, without warning to the United States, Great Britain and the Netherlands Indies. Immediately, for the first time in history, the Pacific Ocean became involved in war; and the conditions of life of every person in the lands in or bordering the Pacific were fundamentally and perhaps permanently changed. Millions of Americans awoke to the horrifying news, that Pearl Harbor had been bombed by Japanese. At that time most people did not know where Pearl Harbor was. However, it wasn't long before every American learned that Pearl Harbor is in Hawaii.

The terrible attack happened at 7:55 A.M., on a Sunday morning; it caught the Naval Fleet stationed at Pearl Harbor, Hawaii off guard. Although there have been rumors that there was a warning in code, it was ignored as a false alarm or something like that.

The attack was by dive-bomber planes and submarines, in less than two hours the attack destroyed or badly damages six battleships, many smaller vessels and over three hundred planes, in addition, about 2,400 Americans lost their lives. It left the United States Navy crippled, and American people shaken.

President Roosevelt in an address on 7 December 1941, said, "A date that will live in infamy" and asked Congress to declare war on Japan. Congress jointly voted on war.

In addition, Congress extended military draft to men; aged 20 to 44 and Admiral Chester Nimitz was appointed United States Pacific Fleet Commander, and Admiral Ernest King was appointed Commander of the United States Navy.

Franklin Delano Roosevelt –"FDR" as he was often called, served as the 32nd president of the United States, born in Hyde Park, New York on 30 January 1882. His fight for causes started long before he became President. A dormitory fire at Harvard when he was editor of the daily "Crimson" spurred him to demand installation of fire-escapes.

FDR served two terms in the New York Senate and joined the ranks of great liberals and social reformers when he was twice governor of the Empire State. He was voted in the nation's highest office and carried out the fight for a "New" deal for the "forgotten man" when he instituted the most sweeping set of measures in the history of the nation to help the jobless, the depressed and underprivileged. His vision carried him beyond the nation's borders. His "good neighbor" policy in the Western Hemisphere, his pleadings and struggles for world peace, and then the war, which he tried so hard to stop, burst upon the world; he became the pivotal statesman of more than thirty United Nations which pooled their might to smash a German Italian-Japanese Axis.

He was America's Chief Executive, and Commander-in-Chief. The only president elected four times. He carried the country through the Great Depression and World War Two, two the the greatest crises this country had ever seen. He also expanded the powers of the federal government through a series of programs and reforms known as the New Deal. And as World War Two was coming to its end, President Roosevelt started slipping away, his fight was over and he was carried away on 12 April 1945 in Warm Springs, Georgia.

On 11 December, Japanese sunk the British Battle Cruiser "Repulse" and the Battleship "Prince of Wales" as they were sailing without air cover, also that same day the Japanese attempted landing on Wake Island, but are pushed back by a Marine detachment.

In the Pacific, the Japanese were winning, even though the United States, Britain and the Netherlands were fighting the best they could. The simple fact was that the Japanese had been planning their attacks for some time. Although Britain was already at war and conscious of the enemy's strategies, the United States was caught off guard.

Although we did have regular Army, Navy, Army Air Force, and Marine Corps units, the majority of American combatants lacked war experience, as they came from the ranks of National Guard units and young men just out of high school.

Back on the World War Two battlefield, General MacArthur's command post, a 1,400-foot-long tunnel on Corregidor was bombed while his army was trapped on the Bataan peninsula. On 22 February 1942, MacArthur was ordered by Roosevelt to withdraw to Australia.

The American and Philippine troops trapped on Bataan were helpless, as their food was gone and their health was deteriorating. On 9 April, General Wainwright ordered a counterattack to the Japanese attack; it proved to be the last.

The next day General Edward P. King and his 79,000 remaining troops surrendered. The troops were taken to Manila, and after being marched through the streets, they were packed in boxcars and forwarded to POW camps. Since the Japanese had more prisoners then they anticipated, (they only counted on 25, 000), the rest could not fit on the boxcars and had to march the sixty-five miles to the camp. The brutal march became known as the "Bataan Death March". An estimated 750 Americans and 5,000 Filipinos had died during the march, and another 16,000 prisoners died within two months of their arrival at camp.

President Roosevelt and his Chiefs of Staff held to the strategy that had been fixed by Churchill before Pearl Harbor. The first objective was the European Theatre and all military supplies were sent there, and the Pacific Theatre had to wait, at Corregidor, General MacArthur waited, and waited, as it happened, for Bataan they did not receive any supplies when they desperately needed them.

On the 18th of April 1942, the United States Armed Forces together attacked Tokyo. The sixteenth Army's B-25 Bombers, under command of Lt. Col., James Doolittle, were loaded on the aircraft carrier Hornet, and transported within 700 miles of Japan. This had been the first time aircraft this large had flown from a carrier deck in war. After the pilots dispersed their bombs the pilots were to fly eleven hundred miles to bases in China to land, because the decks of the carriers were too short for the return landings. However, on their return trip it was night, dark, and raining when they reached the countryside of China. No airfields were visible and the planes were short of fuel, the pilot along with the crews had to parachute out of the planes. Only one plane did not crash land, it landed in Russia.

Women Warriors' during World War Two - Besides and alongside of the men in the Armed Forces are the women that also answered the call to help our country.

At the urging of First Lady Eleanor Roosevelt and women's groups, and impressed by the British use of women in service; in May of 1942, Congress instituted the Women's Auxiliary Army Corps, later upgraded to the Women's Army Corps, which had full military status. Its members known as the WACs, worked in more than 200 non-combating jobs stateside and in every theater of the war. By 1945, there were more than 100,000 WACs and 6,000 female officers in the Navy. Members of Women Accepted for Volunteer Emergency Service (WAVES) held the same status as naval reservist and provided support stateside. The Coast Guard and Marines soon followed suit, though in smaller numbers.

"Rosie the Riveter", the aviation agency saw the greatest number of female workers. More than 310,000 women worked in the U. S. aircraft industry in 1943, representing sixty-five percent of the industry total workforce. The munitions industry also recruited women workers, as represented by the United States government's "Rosie the Riveter" propaganda campaign. The strong bandanna-clad Rosie became one of the most successful recruitment tools in American history, and the most iconic image of working women during World War Two.

In Movies, newspapers, posters, photographs articles, and even in Norman Rockwell-painted Saturday Evening Post cover, the Rosie the Riveter campaign stressed the patriotic need for women to enter the work force—and they did, in huge numbers.

United States Navy Seabees: Most people have never heard about the U. S. Navy Seabees. Before the Navy Seabees were formed, base construction was the province of civilian construction firms that would use contracted or in-house personnel for the requisite design and construction tasks. However, that was to change with the declaration of war on 8 December 1941. The civilian workers could not be sent into harm's way, or carry weapons and the military would need many supply bases throughout the world very quickly.

Admiral Ben Moreell saw this problem coming several weeks before the Japanese bombed Pearl Harbor. His idea was to recruit men with construction skills, put them in uniform, and teach them combat skills. The military liked his idea and soon after Pearl Harbor, the Admiral was authorized to start recruiting for the Navy Construction Battalions.

Initially, the Navy actively solicited enlistees to staff the Seabees, which would be commanded by officers of the Navy's Civil Engineer Corps. Because the military needed skilled and experienced men, the average age of the first Seabee recruits was thirty-seven years. After December 1942 volunteer enlistment was halted for the Seabees, and the Construction Battalions were staffed through the Selective Service System. Afterwards, the average Seabee recruit was much younger and possessed fewer construction skills.

Around the world, the Navy's Seabees established an enviable record for speed and quality of construction under some of the most miserable conditions imaginable. Their "Can Do" spirit was memorialized in the Seabee credo "The difficult, we do immediately, the impossible takes a little longer".

They served in wartime and in peace. Thousands of men came ashore or in country directly behind the invasion troops to build the infrastructure needed for sustained operations against the enemy.

The fact is that much of this wartime infrastructure is still used today, for instance. To most people, Bora, Bora is a Tahitian resort island in the Society Islands chain in the South Pacific. Historically, the island was of great significance to the Allied effort to crush the Japanese during World War II. This tropical paradise was a major supply and support base for the United States military operations in the South Pacific. The buildings, docks, fueling facilities, roads, and airstrips integral to the large military base on this island were among the first accomplishments of the U. S. Navy's famed Construction Battalions, nicknamed the Seabees.

Now the remnants of the Seabee's work have blended into the indigenous features of the island, as the inlanders' wartime English helped them transform their island into an international tourist destination. Bora, Bora was the birthplace of the Seabees.

By September of 1942, attention in the Pacific was at Guadalcanal. The United States Seabees landed on Guadalcanal to develop the airfield. A Navy Seabee veteran named Kenneth Dooley, that I interviewed told me his interesting story about his voyage to Guadalcanal. He said it was the first time for him and most of the boys to ever be aboard a ship, and many of the new sailors were leaning over the railing, feeding the ocean fish for the first few days. Several times they circled the tub for hours, expecting a torpedo to find them before getting started again. After three days they set course westward and when they neared the Island of New Caledonia they attached themselves to a convoy of two other transports, and five warships. Then made a turn and headed north to the Equator.

While out in the ocean, a two-motored bomber flew over daily. The Seabees soon learned it was an ambulance plane bringing casualties from the battle-scarred Solomons, by end of October the convoy hooked-up with five other transports and about nineteen warships. Rumors had it that they were headed for the Solomon's, and even to Guadalcanal. They were all lectured on the wiliness and the treachery of the Japanese who were captured in the Solomon area; it was all quite scary, and all the troops hoped that it was not true.

When Special Seabees made a beachhead on Guadalcanal, the Marines landed first with assault boats and chased the Japanese off the beach. When they saw the signals for the landing boats to come in, the Special Seabee's together with the soldiers went ashore in three waves'. The returning boats from the first wave bought the wounded and the dead back to the ship. For the next few days troops and supplies were unloaded nonstop day and night. The new Seabees soon learned condition "red" meant to dig a foxhole and get into it.

The Seabees primary mission on Guadalcanal was to build an airfield and the engineers went out to find a spot. Condition "red" was called many times during the day and night. The natives on Guadalcanal were at war with the Japanese and often fought alongside of the Marines.

Ken said that one day a widely rumored Japanese task force materialized, reportedly with 40,000 troops. Men of the 14th Special Seabees along with the rest of the troops were given three days of rations, and prepared to make the 35-mile hike through swamp and jungle to Henderson Field on thirty minutes notice.

Fortunately, the enemy force did not have the opportunity to land on Guadalcanal, as it was met offshore by Allied naval forces. A sea battle raged for three days and three nights. Boats were dispatched to pick up sailors, and returned with stories of hundreds of Japanese floating in the water.

On the 9th day of February 1943, the Japanese abandon Guadalcanal after defeat by Americans in long, bitter jungle warfare.

During this same time in the European Theatre side of the war, the Royal Air Force hits Berlin with another series of devastating raids on 2 March.

Around 2 November 1943 after being stationed on the Island for over one year, the 14th Special Seabees received orders that they would embark, and leave the island.

In my books, I am always interested in featuring a veteran of each war, because World War II was in the European and the Pacific Theatres I will feature one in each theatre. In the Pacific battles, I have interviewed about thirty-six Navy Seabees, so I chose to feature a Navy Seabee from the Bronx because he gave me so many interesting stories about what happened to him while fighting the Japanese during World War Two.

Joseph John Garofalo... was born in the Bronx, New York on 15 November 1920. He grew up and attended local schools in the Bronx with his sister. Prior to his military service Joe worked for the Electric Boat Company (ELCO) in Bayonne, New Jersey. Along with the Higgins, ELCO was a primary supplier of Patrol Torpedo (PT) boats to the U. S. Navy. Although his work was essential to the war effort, Joe did not want a strategic deferral and decided to enlist.

Joe tells about his World War Two military experiences: In October 1942, I enlisted in the U. S. Navy Seabees and began basic training at Camp Bradford, Virginia in November. For a 22-year-old city boy, it was culture shock. The conditions were primitive, cold and muddy. We lived in tents with no walkways, just mud. We piled snow against our tents for insulation, and although coal was scarce, we tried to keep warm around one pot-belly-stove in the middle of the tent. Our uniforms did not fit, as every garment was very large. Later, I had my uniforms privately altered.

We trained daily to close order drill, ran the obstacle course, honed our marksmanship on the rifle range, and practiced the basics of demolition and amphibious landings. The Marine drill instructors (D.I.) were on top of us all the time, as they wanted us to be hardened for combat. Some D. I.'s were veterans of Guadalcanal and they relayed their experiences to us. They explained the way the Japanese fight at night as well as the various booby traps that were planted on roads, fields, vehicles and even bodies. At Camp Lejeune and Camp

Pendleton, the training at times was about ten hours a day. That did not include guard duty; K.P. was not very pleasant, and depended on whoever was in charge.

Always I was thinking about the war, and I thought enough to survive. Will I ever become a slacker? How would I react seeing the enemy face to face? All these things went through my mind.

After five weeks, we left Camp Bradford and went on to Camp Endicott in Davisville, Rhode Island; there, we received additional training on the rifle range and practiced close order drill, hikes, and calisthenics. During this time, I had one "liberty" and quickly found a good Italian restaurant in Providence, after enjoying the Italian food, my spirits were lifted, and feeling more fit and seasoned than when I started. Afterwards, our battalion was then divided in half.

Our half went to Port Hueneme, California, and my half was shipped to Camp Lejeune, North Carolina for advanced training. We then became the 121st Seabees as part of the 4th Marine Division on 10 May 1943. After a few months at Lejeune, we departed to Camp Pendleton, California. Once there we were given more advanced training in amphibious maneuvers, bridge building, marksmanship, demolition and the obstacle course.

In January 1944, we left San Diego, California sailing on the USS Wayne for 10-11 days. Our Battalion landed on 1 February 1944 on the Japanese held Kwajalein Island Roi-Namur in the Marshall Islands Group. Prior to disembarking, we were waiting to climb down on nets to LCVP's; it started to get light and foggy.

I was looking at the ocean staring and thinking, the worst. Suddenly, I saw something floating towards our ship – I could not make it out. A few minutes later, I saw a raft with three figures. My buddies, and I saw this and we immediately started firing, as the men on the raft were Japanese. At the same time a transport crew member opened fire on the raft with a 20mm cannon. One of the Japanese on the raft was hit and his body flipped into the air. Finally, all three were killed. The Japanese had charges designed to adhere to the hull of our transport and destroy it. That experience was our baptism of fire, even before our landing on Roi-Namur, (Kwajalein). Hundreds of Marines climbed down nets to get on LCVP Higgins boats.

We were very seasick in the landing boat. When we hit the beach, Renato Bianchi pulled me off the boat and into a shell hole on the beach, as we were under fire. Commander John Partridge was "scared for life", and asked me to find his pack while we were being shot at. I did not really look too hard for it.

A sniper had us pinned down when the company commander crawled under me to avoid being hit, raising my body into the line of fire. I figured that I would be killed anyway, so I stood up and emptied the fifteen rounds from my carbine into the tree. The body of the sniper fell from the tree onto the ground with a dull thump. As the marines advanced across the island, firing began to subside after a few hours. The island was secured in about two days.

The Seabees designated as marine engineers worked on a causeway on Roi-Namur. On the second or third day a powerful explosion flung me about four feet in the air; debris was still coming down a minute later. Apparently, 20 marines had thrown a charge into a Jap bunker that was filled with torpedo heads. A second group of marines was going to do the same when they were interrupted by the detonation of the first bunker. The large crater that resulted was below the water table and quickly filled with water. After the island was secured, we went to Maui in the Hawaiian Islands, where we rested and underwent further training for the next three months.

JOE the NAVY SEABEE

On 15 June 1944, we landed on Saipan from LCVP landing craft. Our objective was to land on Blue-Beach-2, which was to the right of the Japanese sugar mill smokestack, as stated on the mimeograph sketch that was given to us.

Hundreds of landing craft were rendezvousing, waiting for the signal to head for their designated landing beach. Moments later our craft was alone, only ten men were in our LCVP because we were carrying ammunition. We were headed towards Tinian, the wrong island, which was three miles to the south of Saipan. I looked at my sketch, and then looked up and saw Saipan disappearing. I told Chief Sullivan (who was in charge of our platoon on board), "Chief, we are headed for the wrong island".

Suddenly, I saw the coxswain staring into space, frozen at the wheel. We realized that he was in shock and we were headed for Tinian the wrong island. One of our men heard me shout at the Chief and quickly slapped the coxswain in his face. Just as he recovered the Japanese artillery on Tinian opened fire on us. Two shells came very close to us. The craft almost capsized; we were taking on water. As we turned away heading for Saipan, one shell exploded in our wake. This was very close, even if you were a good swimmer, you would have never made it. The gear and treacherous currents would have drowned all of us. We made it to Saipan and there we encountered deadly artillery fire on the beach.

Fear played havoc on Saipan during "D" Day. I saw men on the beach crying and calling out to their mother, while others pounded the sand and prayed aloud. Others swam off the island and drowned. It was a sight that I will never forget. The Japanese artillery was devastating.

Tony Mellino was in charge of our detail on Saipan. I was told to sling my carbine around my neck so that I could push a wagon loaded with belted ammunition with both hands. One man pulled, while I was in the back pushing. Two men with Thompsons and two men with carbines escorted us, and assisted in pushing the wagon.

Suddenly, all hell broke loose. The wagon stopped and our escorts scattered. I went around the wagon and saw a Japanese soldier coming at me, wearing only a jock strap and a helmet. He had already hit the hand grenade plunger on his helmet to activate it. As I tried to remove my carbine, I saw bullet holes appear on his chest with smoke rings coming out. The men that scattered had taken cover and opened fire on him. He fell on his own grenade and the force of the explosion lifted his body about two feet above the ground. Shrapnel hit the ammunition and the wagon as the body landed approximately six feet from me. This was another close encounter.

At that time a Navy corpsman took me aside and insisted that I drink some whiskey. Reality hit me later when I realized what had happened. Later that afternoon, I was bringing the wounded back when a Japanese machine gunner opened up on us. I landed on top of a Marine. The machine gunner sprayed continuously. The bullets just missed my back by inches. I could see the bullets hitting a wall. I told the Marine below me to exhale. I thought that was the end. However, it was not, as the Japanese machine gunner was killed moments later.

Once on patrol, I discovered a group of Japanese soldiers. I heard their voices and actually smelled their pungent odor. Upon my return from patrol, I reported this to Lt. Robert Fiske, and the 121st Seabees and units of the 4th Marine Division were alerted, and when 200 Japanese attacked an hour later, they were all killed. For my role in this action in filling the gap between two front line companies, I was recommended for the Bronze Star.

Saipan – D-Plus 2 the beaches on Saipan were still under attack from Japanese artillery. Many fallen Marines that had died since D-Day were still on the beaches due to conditions that existed. The battalion chaplain was begging for volunteers to help remove the bodies from the beaches for sea burial. Many men were asked to perform this task, but they could not handle it. I and two other men volunteered. I climbed into a LVT (track vehicle), which had built-in-shelves to hold bodies that would be transported to a ship for this purpose. The two men would pick up a body and hand it to me, which I would slide on a shelf. Prior to sliding the body in place, it had to lean on me in order to be put on a shelf.

Blood from wounds were all over my jacket. I was saturated throughout. I was attacked by green and yellow flies. They were all over my jacket. I was a terrible sight for anyone to see. Seabees and Marines were pouring water all over my jacket and used knives to cut the jacket off me. To this day, I still get recurrences of that day. This happened 62 years ago. It is still vivid in my mind.

The first day in Saipan we sustained 2,000 casualties. The second day it reached 3,500. Most of the casualties were at the front line resulting from deadly artillery, snipers and stray fire. At night, the Japanese probed for gaps in the Marine lines and counter-attacked many times. For the first three days they weren't very effective, but we suffered quite a few casualties from these counterattacks. The 5" star shells that illuminated the island saved us many nights.

On 18 June, the U. S. ships pulled away from Saipan and left us stranded without supplies, water and fire support. The ship left to engage large elements of the Japanese Navy. The ship joined a task force led by Admiral Marc Mitscher that eventually destroyed 400 Japanese planes in 24 hours. The Japanese pilots were young and inexperienced compared to the U. S. Pilots.

In July 1944, the 121st Seabees were the first navel construction outfit to land on Tinian. Other units came later fully equipped. The army units came in with their equipment. For a few weeks, we managed to infiltrate the army chow lines, but that eventually ended.

About a month since our landing on Tinian, I contracted dengue fever. I was flown in a C-47 to an Army hospital facility on Saipan where I laid on a cot for ten days, then was flown back to Tinian.

We worked on the airfield on Tinian for five months, and subsisted for almost three months exclusively on C-rations. Coral blasted from high points on the island was used to fill in depressions to make runways. Coral was deposited in thirty inch layers, watered, and rolled again and again to achieve the needed compaction to support landing and takeoff by heavily laden bombers.

After months of hardship on Tinian, we finally had tents erected as living quarters. The Seabees devised a wind-powered washing machine mostly from Japanese bicycle parts. The machines featured a windmill-driven plunger in a bucket to create the agitation needed to clean our clothes. It was quite a sight to see a number of these wind-driven washing machines operating all at the same time.

Our thoughts of home were now displaced by our current reality. We thought about the lives we left behind only when we received letters and photographs from home. Our concerns were put into perspective by the insensitive marine colonel on the transport who would pointedly tell us before each operation, "a lot of you men are not coming back". Comments like those, along with Tokyo Rose playing favorite hit tunes on the air would really bother us.

Most of our work on Tinian was on the North Field, the largest construction project of the war. At that time, the airfield we built on Tinian was considered the largest airfield in the world. Over 14,000 Seabees worked on North and West Field, periodically on North Field, I operated a steamroller.

The strangest job that was assigned to me was to work with Jack Ovies to get rid of frogs that were in the drainage ditch around the perimeter of Ushi Field, Tinian. We had to shovel them out of the ditch by the thousands as they were obstructing water flow. The nightmare was also mentioned in our 1946 Battalion history book.

While on Saipan in August 1945, I was awakened by a friend who stated that a large new bomb was dropped on Japan. A few days later, we were informed that the war was over.

Although we never knew about the Manhattan Project, the 121st Seabees worked on the buildings that housed the atomic bombs, dug the atomic bomb pits on North Field, and built the runways used by the B-29 bombers involved in the raids on Hiroshima and Nagasaki, the Enola Gay and Bockscar flew over our heads.

While visiting Saipan on the anniversary of the invasion, Joe spotted this oxygen tank at a church entrance; the tank was a relic of WWII, they had cut out the bottom and were using it for a bell. Joe was so fascinated that the Pastor offered it to him; he told me a long story about taking it home.

Many years after the war, Joe felt his community was not doing enough to remember our nation's veterans and set out with his friend of forty-five years, Angelo Pinto, a war historian and collector, to create the Bronx Veterans Museum.

Joe has the tank on display at his museum that he created for the World War Two veterans in the Bronx, New York. I visited the museum that Joe created; it is in the foyer of a funeral parlor. Joe had asked for space in the local library of his home town, the Bronx, but the library refused and the funeral parlor welcomed it. There is a plaque on the front of the red brick building that dedicated the museum to the veterans of World War Two, and also states that it was founded by Joe Garofalo.

Joe was discharged from the United States Navy Seabees in November 1945, during the war; he had corresponded with a nice looker that he met at a dance before he went into the service. In June 1948, Lillian and Joe got married. They had two wonderful sons and four granddaughters.

Joe Garofalo, passed away on 13 March 2016. He was ninety-five years old.

While the Navy Seabees and some Marine Divisions were fighting the Japanese in the Pacific, the other side of the world Hitler's war was still raging in Europe.

In January the Germans begin to withdraw from the Caucasus and the Soviets begin in the offensive against the Germans in Stalingrad; Montgomery's Eighth Army takes Tripoli and the first bombing raids by Americans on Germany (at Wilhelmshaven).

On 2 February 1943, Germans surrender at Stalingrad in the first big defeat of Hitler's armies. The battle of Atlantic climaxes with 27 merchant ships sunk by German U-boats, and by the end of March Montgomery's Eighth Army breaks through the Mareth (a region of N. Africa) Line in Tunisia.

D-Day, 6 June 1944: Better known as the Normandy Invasion.

Planning of the D-Day Invasion (Overlord) was first secretly discussed at Tehran, the capital of Iran, during a conference meeting in late November of 1943. The Allied power was swelling and Germany's armies were dwindling everywhere. The big three, Roosevelt, Churchill and Stalin had flown in from separate countries to meet for the first time in Tehran for the conference.

In the spring of 1942, Britain and America had been working on various plans for many months, but neither the troops nor technical equipment existed for such a large operation to be a success, they were especially short of war ships and landing craft. Washington and London both agreed that France should be the target for a larger assault. At the meeting in late winter, President Roosevelt and Churchill agreed that General Eisenhower should be in command of the Channel Invasion named, Overlord.

In March 1944, Eisenhower set up his headquarters in England to take command of the Supreme Headquarters for the Allied Expeditionary Force. After consulting with logistical and meteorological experts, and going over repeatedly with maps, the decision was that the invasion would take place along some sixty miles of beaches along Normandy's Cotentin Peninsula. In order to prevent the Germans from supplying their armies with provisions, on the northern front of France by rail and air; the American bombers destroyed the French railroads and bridges. In Northern France, there was not a bridge in existence to support the German Panzer tanks.

In Britain, the men involved assembled, the sailors, soldiers, and pilots curiously planned and rehearsed for the invasion. The force was two-million strong with a substantial supply of weapons to support them. The final date set for the invasion was 5 June 1944, the beaches east of the Cherbourg peninsula in Normandy is where the landing would take place.

Montgomery was to handle the ground forces at Normandy, later Generals Bradley, Paton, Joe Collins, and Courtney Hodges would take their armies for the advance through France, and Monty command the Brits and Canadian Twenty-first army.

The Allied armies had to do a lot of building to prepare the beaches for the landings, because the Germans had destroyed the harbor. A pipe line was built under the ocean channel in order to supply the thousands of gallons of fuel needed to support the troops machinery, the fuel was pumped through every day to keep the armies on the move.

The allied forces built their own harbors, they built what are known as Mulberries, built with steel and concrete, and then the seven miles of piercing was towed from England as prefabricated units. Each artificial harbor weighed 750,000 tons and had the capacity of about the port of Dover. They did this from hollow concrete and then towed them over to Normandy and sunk them end to end to build a pier. Timing was important; every detail had been planned; the short summer nights, the tides.

On the 4th day of June, the weather did not look good; high winds, and stormy seas were expected, and the ski was cloudy. Therefore, the landing postponed. Tension started to build as the forces waited another twenty-four hours. Then the weather improved and the decision was made by Supreme Commander Eisenhower for the landing to take place on the morning of 6 June, and the orders were relayed to the allied forces.

All on the South Coast of England, the forces started moving like a long train, the citizens of England watched in awe. Some were crying as their loved ones waved good-bye, never knowing if they would see them again. They left the harbors, heading for Normandy. A few hours after the ground troops got underway, the airborne troops took off in order to land just before the invasion.

After several hours the news reports of the invasion started coming in.

The airborne, B-17's late arrival and cloud cover forced them to release their bombs well inland from the beach. No bombs hit the beach or bluff as planned. The beach invasion was under the cover of clouds and the Germans were not aware and taken by surprise. Because of the weather the Germans did not expect the invasion and Rommel, who was in charge of the German forces had gone to Germany to visit Hitler.

The first landing on Utah Beach was at 6:10 A.M. the least costly invasion to the Allies on D-Day, with fewer than 200 causalities and 23,500 troops landed. 28 out of 32 tanks made it to shore. Omaha Beach landed at 6:30 A.M. was the hardest hit, causalities on the beaches and in the landing crafts was heavy, and the worst fighting occurred on the left flank where the Americans were next to the Brits sector.

At 7:30 A.M. the landing was at Gold Beach, the most successful of the landings on D-Day, 25,000 men landed with only 400 casualties. At 8:00 A.M. Sword Beach landed successfully with 29,000 British troops and just over 600 casualties. And at 8:0 5A.M. after being delayed by rough seas the Canadians landed on Juno Beach, the Canadians suffered a total of 1,200 casualties out of a force of 21,400. They made the furthest penetration inland of the Allies.

By dawn, the German artillery started hitting the beaches in full. Little-by-little the Germans were driven back and about a fifty-mile front had been gained by the Allied Forces. The "Mulberries", served well, over five-thousand ships and landing craft took part in the invasion, and when the English Commander Churchill visited the Normandy beach one week later, he described it as a city of ships.

Germany, Hitler captured the citizen's hope by telling them about his new fighting machine. On 13 June, one week after D-day, the first flying bomb hit England.

On 9-10 July Allies land in Sicily and by 12-17 August Germans evacuate Sicily. In early September, the Italians surrendered.

One of the biggest bombing raids during the war took place on 24 July 1943, after the Allied Forces were taking a heavy beating from the Luftwaffe bombing and German U-boats. The American and British Royal Air Forces agreed completely on the need for a massive air offensive to cripple the enemy. The Allies put a plan together for the bombing of Germany's industrial areas, the first point of target being the port of Hamburg where half the manufacturing of U-boats took place.

On that night, 24 July, about seven hundred and forty bombers in successive waves bombed for two hours. That was the beginning, the next ten days the Americans bombed by day and the Royal Air Force bombed by night. Then in December 1943, the P-51 Mustang appeared, a fighter with combat radius from its base, with drop tanks, 850 miles.

With this advantage, the war turned to the Allies favor. By D-Day, the Luftwaffe was shattered.

Hitler's new weapon became known as V-bombs, flying without a pilot, it was controlled, they were small carrying a large load of explosives and flown in a course set by internal mechanism. When the course was completed the engine stopped, and the flying bomb fell to earth with a deadly explosion. The people of London learned to listen for its buzzing sound and be able to find cover. They called them "buzz bombs" or "doodle bombs". They did do a lot of damage to London, and they did kill people and cause hardships, but they did not win the war.

Soon after the so-called V-bombs, Hitler's regime came up with a newer bomb, this one they named the V2s bombs, they were high-speed rockets, and they rose fifty miles into the air at a speed of nearly four thousand miles an hour. They landed in London, with no warning of their arrival; the first sign was an explosion. Fortunately, Germany could not produce many of them.

After three weeks of siege in Cherbourg it fell to the Americans. When living up to his nick-name, "Lighting Joe", General Joe Collins was able to capture Cherbourg with his forces around 26 of June, although the Germans reduced the port to ruins before they surrendered.

In the city of Caen in Northern France, Canadian and British Army's were being attacked by German armored divisions until the end of June, when the Allied attacks leveled the city. Afterward General Crerar marched his army to Falsies where upon arrival found more devastation, not a single house was standing and the people of the village were hiding in the forest. The local French Freedom Fighters assisted General Patton, with the Third Army and marched through the point and south through Brittany at end of July.

Hitler's Generals wanted him to surrender his armies because they knew that Germany was losing the war, but Hitler refused. Soon after Hitler escaped with little injuries on 17 July, an attack was made on his life; when an officer placed a briefcase with a bomb in it against the table where he had been sitting as he addressed a conference. Four officials sitting at the table were killed, several high-ranking German officers shared in the plot.

When General Patton's forces came up the peninsula from Brittany, a region and province of NW France, between the English

Channel and the Bay of Biscay they drove the German forces to the north and the British forces closed in from the north, the Germans were cut off and trapped in a swelling pocket. The pocket was then closed by the Canadians; Major Currie with only one-hundred-seventy-five men anchored the German's escape until reinforcements arrived. The allied air power arrived in time to prevent anymore counter attacks.

Early August, American and French forces surrounded the city of Paris, following General Eisenhower's orders not to let the city be destroyed by the Germans. Inside the city the French patriots battled against the Nazis until an armored division advanced into the center of Paris and accepted the German officer's surrender.

Now it is fall, Belgium and Luxembourg are emancipated and the Nazis are driven back, and the Allies' ground troops are moving toward the Rhine in Germany. At this stage of the war, the Allied armies are getting short of rations and other supplies.

The British Army at the Belgian-Dutch frontier are halted at the three rivers, the Waal, Meuse and the lower Rhine, the bridges over the rivers are guarded by German guards. Field Marshal Montgomery devises a way to seize the bridges; he called on the Allied air support.

On 17 September the airborne units took off from England, they were dropped down and after difficult fighting at Eindhoven and Nijmegen they captured the two bridges. At Arnhem, the first day, U. S. Dakota's dropped three British parachute battalions and landed two hundred and ninety-seven gliders.

The parachutes were put down out-side of the city and almost immediately found resistance. They were fighting their way with the help of Dutch patriots with little headway. The second parachute battalion was able to obtain a footing on the bridge but while waiting for three days for reinforcement they were either killed or captured.

The rest of the airborne forces were either scattered throughout the city or captured and under conditions of hardship and lack of supplies by the eighth day, General Urquhart withdrew the river crossing. The plan had failed with the loss of thousands of men.

On the other hand, the advance by the Americans to the Nijmegen Bridge was held, and at a bitter cost allowed the Allied troops to leap into Germany.

When the port of Antwerp opened, supplies for the Allies were able to reach them and the forces began planning their attack on Germany.

The Allied army was able to attack the Germans on all sides and with the overhead Allied bombers assault; you would think that the Nazis would surrender.

But the Americans first army assault did not stop the Germans; 10 December, 1945, there was a vicious attack on the Allies who were shrinking in number over the Ardennes, the attack was a surprise. A quick response from the Allies as they regrouped their armies and much to their surprise were magically supported by the 7th Armored Division who had halted the Panzer Division at St. Vith. History has it that when General Tony McAuliffe was given the command to surrender by the Nazis, he replied with the word "Nuts" and continued fighting. To this day the word "Nuts" is used by the people of Bastogne as meaning defiance.

It appears that the "Battle of the Bulge" was given its name when the Germans operation pushed forward about fifty-miles toward the Meuse, a very perilous territory. At this point the Germans were pushed back and beaten, and Brussels and Antwerp were no longer threatened. Air support also was successful after bombing German airfields and destroying the Germans two-hundred aircraft on 1 January, 1945.

As the German armies dug in on the Gothic Line; a defensive position extending across Italy from coast to coast. The Allied armies attacked the Gothic Line in September, 1945. They were making great headway until constant rains filled the valleys and they were not able to move the big guns through.

The Fifth and Eighth Italian Armies fought hard, they were short of men and unable to make the landing force for the South of France. After each advance they were halted rapidly by another mountain range or new river.

At last, in April the Germans mountain stronghold and all supplies were destroyed by a blazing air attack, and the Allied armies marched through the Gothic Line and scattered the enemy. The partisans that had hidden in the mountains hurriedly joined the Allied army as they went from town to town capturing them from the Nazi garrisons.

On 25 April, Mussolini was captured when he was trying to escape to Switzerland dressed in a German uniform. The partisan patrol recognized him and arrested him. He was shot and his body was sent to Milan where it was placed on exhibit in the market place on meat hooks, by his feet.

Meanwhile, General Clark's Fifth Army had successfully passed its test at Salerno and now drove on to Naples, the most important single prize in South Italy. The Germans, fighting a skilled defense did not bother to defend the city, taking vengeance for Italy's defection, smashed it and withdrew northward. The Americans and Brits entered Naples on 1 October 1944, they found the port and everything within three-hundred yards of it had been destroyed by the Nazis.

The natives of Naples gave the Allied armies a grand welcome; they had been starved and frightened by looters. The American engineers did what they could to restore the city from the wreckage.

In early 1945 the Allies regrouped for what was known as the final drive through Germany. In order to get to the German homeland, they had to cross the Rhine River that was wide and deep. Gathering the forces to attack on the central front was General Bradley, in the north, the British Twenty-First Army Group, in the south the French First Army stood on the side of the Americans. The Germans continued fighting while driven back as they retreated across the Rhine they blew up the bridges behind them.

The Germans were taken by surprise when they failed to collapse one of the bridges over the river. On 7 March General Bradley found the bridge intact, and was able to cross five divisions before it was discovered by the Germans and they bombed it. But the rest of the troops were already putting together pontoon bridges to finish the crossing.

The northern armies swept around the Ruhr and joined hands with General Bradley's forces, and on 18 April the entire Ruhr garrison surrendered. The industrial heart of Germany had stopped beating.

On 12 April, President Roosevelt died. He had steered his country through the perilous years with unfailing faith and courage. It was a tragedy that he did not live to see the final victory. Although he knew that, at least in Europe, it was near. Americans all over the world mourned a gallant leader, and in every Allied county the people felt that they had lost a loyal friend and powerful force in the cause of freedom.

Vice President Truman became president and carried on the grand alliance. The Nazi front in the west had collapsed, and the routed German forces gave themselves up in hordes to escape capture by the Russians, whose vengeance they feared more. The Allied armies swept on, liberating their own prisoners as they went.

The stark horror of the concentration camps was revealed, and the Allied troops were greeted by throngs of starved and tortured human beings. Medical teams took over the camps to care for the living and bury the dead.

Germen Concentration Camps….. In Axis prisons, before Germany could hide the evidence that convicted it of war crimes. The American, British and Russian troops witnessed the torture chambers of the Nazis, and the savagery of the accused. Disregarding the Geneva Convention, the Allies found camp after camp filled with men of all Allied Armies, most in poorest of health.

It is a matter of history that when Supreme Commander of the Allied Forces, General Dwight Eisenhower, found the victims of the death camps, he ordered all possible photographs to be taken, and for the German people from surrounding villages to be ushered through the camps and even made to carry each corps one and one half miles to be buried. I think it was a good educational treatment, many of the civilian Germans say they were not aware of what went on, "This I do not believe" in those days freight cars of dead bodies on railroad sidings. It is a terrible page in history of the human race.

The largest camp was Moosburg, in Bavaria, liberated by the Third Army, it contained 110,000 prisoners. In all the camps the same suffering of the men occurred. They were forced to march for hundreds of miles with trench feet. Bread and water twice a day was common on forced marches, lice and bedbugs filled their beds, disgustingly inedible food…threats of death were constant and brutal torture, prisoners no longer strong enough to work and had fallen, were picked-up and screaming tossed into the furnaces alive. Those that visited the camp expressed them as **horrible**, physical and mental torture, hell hole of diabolic torture, inhumane suffering.

Six American flyers were clubbed to death, by a dozen German civilians. These men had parachuted from a crippled plane and been captured. They were being taken, under a loose guard to a prison camp, when the men and women of the mob wrested them from their captors.

At Belsen Camp, one of the worst torture houses was among the first to be overrun. Soldiers of the British Second Army could not believe the thing they saw there, the terrible stories they heard from the victims who had survived the Holocaust. Naked men and women were forced to parade for hours in winter rains; other prisoners, fully clothed, were turned into locked compounds with vicious dogs, made half-wild by deliberate starvation. Vivisection on prisoners was common. Women were flogged on their breasts. Men and women alike were lashed on the sensitive soles of their feet. Attractive women were compelled to submit to love-making of their captors

In all the Concentration Camps survivors were suffering from starvation, typhoid, tuberculosis and typhus. And, large piles of unburied corpses lay everywhere stripped of all clothing. In the prison camps there were piles of untouched Red Cross packages that the officials deprived their captures of.

The Geneva Convention provides that prisoners, while they may be put to work with wages, must not be employed in war industries. The Germans violated this ban daily; they forced their captures into slave labor in mines for as much as ten hours every day of every week, on a diet of bread and water with a sauce of beatings with picks if they faltered at their work.

So, cherish – what we have and pray and live so that our children will never be faced with a similar situation.

By January, Hitler had moved his headquarters from the Wolf's Lair in East Prussia to Berlin. Years before, at the height of his power, he had built himself the Chancellery, a majestic and luxurious setting for supreme dictators, ruler of a great nation. Now it stood in the center of a ruined city, and he lived in a deep concrete bunker in the garden.

Before he died, Hitler made a last statement to the German citizens filled with his old hatred of the Jews. He expressed no shame and no regrets. He had not changed since he lived in the slums of Vienna, but he had dragged the German people down to the lowest depths of disaster.

Hitler did not live to face his judges, he chose the easier way out.

Hitler married Eva Braun, when she had joined him in the bunker. On the 30th day of April 1945, he poisoned his dog and his wife. Then he shot himself.

On 7 May, the German Commander in Chief, Field Marshal Wilhelm Keitel, Hitler's yes-man signed an unconditional surrender at Zhukov's headquarters in 1945, to the representatives of America, Britain, France, and Russia. On the 12th May 1945, the last shots in Europe had been fired ending the war in Europe that lasted for five years and eight months. The war in Europe was ended. Keitel was condemned and executed at the trials in Nuremberg in 1946.

OKINAWA: The war against Japan still had to be won. On 1 April 1945, two weeks after the fall of Iwo Jima, American forces attacked Okinawa in the Ryukyu Island chain; approximately three - hundred - forty - eight miles south of Japan. By this time small units of the British fleet had joined the Americans in the pacific. It was a massive attack...thirteen-hundred ships under the command of Vice-Admiral Richard Turner backed up the landing, with combined Allied air bombardment.

Amphibian tanks, guarded by gunboats, began the long parade of landings on Okinawa's beaches; Amtrak's delivering Marine Divisions, Army Unit forces and more tanks. As the troops moved cautiously on and inward on the beaches, the enemy lay low. There was no opposing party in sight, by dusk there was more than sixty-thousand troops ashore, and still all was quiet, no enemy in sight, in fact, there was little opposition anywhere. After five days passed, the Marines uttered that Okinawa was the most messed-up place in the Pacific, with its valleys filled with up-side down masses of boulders, small paths and thick brush everywhere.

Suddenly, as the landing forces moved further inland and reached the Japanese first offense line, all action broke out. The Japanese army sprung-out of fortified positions in the craggy terraces, from honeycombed hills and bombproof caves. At the same time the Marines were also pounded by task forces flown in from air fields in Japan and Okinawa with about seven-hundred aircraft, including three-hundred-fifty kamikazes. The suicide planes crashed down among the ships.

The fighting and the dying went on and on, for days and weeks, as they fought from one mass of boulders in valleys to another, all crawling with Japanese. As they went from cave to cave, it was a battle of bloody butchery and torment, battles ending with knives, bayonets and grenades.

The most fiercely defended position was in the ancient city of Shuri, there marine flamethrowers burned their way through dugouts in immemorial cemeteries. When the last strongpoint on Kiiyama fell, approximately one-hundred-ten-thousand-seventy-one Japanese were dead, nine for every American. Before dawn on 22 June 1945, Japanese Ushijima and his principal subordinate, Lit. Gen. Cho knelt in full dress uniform before their headquarters cave and cut out their entrails. Finally the resistance on the entire island came to an end. Approximately eleven-thousand Japanese surrendered.

Eighty-two days later, the American forces won the battle, and as the remnants of the defeated Japanese army crowded to the water banks they were called out to surrender, instead most of them held grenades to their stomachs and committed suicide in a tribute to their Emperor. Okinawa ended the battles in the Pacific.

As the American flag was raised over Okinawa, prayers were said for the twelve-thousand-five-hundred Americans that lost their lives in the battle. Among them were General Bruckner and American correspondent Ernie Pyle.

"We are with them when they enlist in the great army of freedom, we see them past with those they love. Robert G. Ingersoll"

American scientists had completed the final testing of the Atomic Bomb by July 1945. The making of it was top secret, while the final tests were being done at the New Mexico Desert, the Allied Air support and ground troops were training for an all out invasion on Japan.

I spoke with a United States Air Force veteran who told me that he was really scared while training for the invasion and making maneuvers (practicing), because he was only seventeen years of age and one-hundred-thirteen pounds, and was a tail gunner in the turret of a B-17. Everyone knows that back then if the plane was hit that the tail gunner had no way out. He said, that when he heard that the Atomic Bomb had been dropped, he cried, he was so relieved, because they did not have to proceed with the bombing.

The Japanese government was divided, when the Potsdam warning arrived, the Emperor and some of his more humane ministers wished to surrender, but the other warriors were determined to fight to the end.

Meanwhile the Allied air support had dropped millions of leaflets in order to spare the lives of civilians. For ten days the allies waited for signs of surrender, with no response.

On 26 July 1945, the horrible fate of the heavy cruiser Indianapolis and the crew that had dropped anchor at Tinian in the Mariana's, and after a brief stay the warship departed for the Philippines. Three days out the cruiser while traveling unescorted across the Philippine Sea to join a training unit off Leyte Gulf was sunk by torpedoes from the Japanese submarine 1-58. Of the 1,200 men aboard, barely 300 would live to learn that the cargo they had left behind on Tinian contained the components of the first Atomic Bomb to be dropped on Japan.

On 6 August 1945, a Superfortress, B-29, nick-name the Enola Gay (after Tibbets mother), piloted by Col. Paul W. Tibbets, Jr. and two observers (B-29s) flew from Tinian Island to Japan. The bomb was the result of scientists work, named the "Manhattan Project", created and designed in the United States and tested in Alamogordo, New Mexico. The nine-thousand pound bomb was dropped on the industrial city of Hiroshima, Japan. The death count was estimated about one-hundred-forty-thousand.

Three days later, 9 August 1945, a second bomb was dropped on Nagasaki, Japan; the second plane also took off from Tinian Island, and was piloted by Major Charles W. Sweeney. It was an earth shaking blast that sent a mushroom boiling up to 50,000 feet. Sixty percent of the city had been destroyed with 86,000 inhabitants killed and 61,000 injured; the United States estimated that about 20, 000 were school children. The planes and the crews returned to Tinian Island safely.

On the 15th day of August the Emperor for the time addressed his people directly, telling him that Japan must accept defeat. The war in the Far East was ended. The news of the Japanese surrender spread quickly and miraculously peace had come to the entire Allies' countries.

On the 2nd day of September 1945, General Douglas MacArthur, Supreme Commander for the Allied Powers, along with Admiral Nimitz and representatives of other Allied nations stood at attention aboard the great Battleship Missouri at Tokyo Bay receiving and signing of the unconditional surrender from two Japanese envoys, Mamoru Shigemitsu, representing the Emperor and the government, and Yoshihito Umezu, representing the Imperial Armed Forces.

Also anchored in Tokyo Bay were two-hundred-fifty-eight warships of all types from battleships to beaching craft, representing the Allied nations that had been at war against the Japanese.

Dwight D. Eisenhower: At this section of my book I would like to introduce you to Dwight David Eisenhower, the military warrior that I have chosen from the European Theater during World War Two to feature in my book.

Dwight Eisenhower was born on 14 October 1890, in a small town in Texas, named Denison. In June of 1911, Eisenhower entered into the United States Military Academy; Eisenhower had an astonishing

1912 football touchdown praised by the New York Herald. A week after sharing a tackle of Jim Thorpe, Eisenhower's sports career ended with a severe knee injury. Due to that injury Eisenhower prayed it would not keep him out of the military.

He graduated in 1915 from the Academy sixty-first in a class of one-hundred-sixty-four. With his commission, the Army offered to assign him to the coast artillery, but Eisenhower viewed it as offering it due to his knee injury and the position offered a minimum of excitement and he preferred to become a civilian. West Point's chief medical officer interceded with the War; Conner quickly helped Eisenhower to be assigned to the American Battle Monuments Commission, directed by General John J. Pershing, in Washington. Despite not having participated in the battles within six months Eisenhower produced a "Guide to the American Battle Fields in Europe," an excellent overview of the United States' participation in World War One.

The research made Eisenhower perhaps the army's best expert on Pershing's strategies during the war other than Conner and Pershing himself, and was a thorough preparation for his World War II duties. Pershing wrote a letter praising Eisenhower, and from then on the army saw him as one of its future leading officers.

He was assigned to the Army War College, and then served as executive officer to Major General George Van Horn Moseley, Assistant Secretary of War, from 1929 to 1933. He then served as chief military aide to General Douglas MacArthur, Chief of Staff of the United States Army, until 1935, when he accompanied MacArthur to the Philippines, where he served as assistant military advisor to the Philippine government.

Eisenhower was promoted to lieutenant colonel in 1936. Eisenhower returned to the United States in late December 1939 and held a series of staff positions in Washington, D.C., California and Texas. He served as regimental executive officer of the 15th Infantry at Fort Lewis, Washington. Late in 1940 he became Chief of staff of the 3rd Infantry Division- Fort Lewis. In June 1941 Eisenhower was appointed Chief of Staff to General Walter Krueger, Commander of the Third U. S. Army, at Fort Sam Houston. In San Antonio, Texas he was promoted to Brigadier General in September 1941.

After the Japanese attacked Pearl Harbor Eisenhower served until June 1942, his responsibility was creating the major war plans to defeat

Germany and Japan. In the first days of the war he had been appointed Deputy Chief in charge of Pacific Defenses under the Chief of War Plans Division, General Leonard T. Gerow, and then succeeded Gerow as Chief of the War Plans Division. Then he was appointed Assistant Chief of Staff in charge of Operations Division under Army Chief of Staff General George Marshall.

It was his close association with Marshall that finally brought Eisenhower to senior command positions. Marshall recognized his great organizational and administrative skills.

In 1942 Eisenhower was appointed Commanding General, European Theater of Operations, United States Army (ETOUSA) and was based in London, England. In November he was also appointed Supreme Commander Allied Expeditionary Force of the North African Theater of Operations, U. S. Army. The word expeditionary was dropped soon after his appointment for security reasons.

In February 1943, his authority was extended as commander of AFHQ across the Mediterranean basin to include the British Eighth Army, commanded by General Bernard Law Montgomery. The Eighth Army had advanced across the western desert from the east and was ready for the start of the Tunisia campaign.

Eisenhower gained his fourth star and gave up command of ETOUSA to be commander of NATOUSA. After the capitulation of Axis forces in North Africa, Eisenhower remained in command of the renamed Mediterranean theater of operations, keeping the operational title and continued in command of NATOUSA renamed MTOUSA. In this position he oversaw the allied invasion of Sicily and the Allied invasion of Italy.

It was announced in 1943, that Eisenhower would be Supreme Allied Commander in Europe. In January 1944, he resumed command of European Theater of Operations, United States Army (ETOUSA), and the following month was officially designated as the Supreme Allied Commander of the Allied Expeditionary Force, serving in a dual role until the end of hostilities in Europe in May 1945.

NORMANDY INVASION – June 1944 In these positions he was charged with planning and carrying out the Allied assault on the coast of Normandy in June 1944 under the code name Operation Overlord, the liberation of Western Europe and invasion of Germany. From then until the end of World War II in Europe on 8 May 1945, Eisenhower through SHAEF had supreme command of all operational allied forces and through his command of ETOUSA, also administrative command of all U. S. forces on the Western Front. As recognition of his senior position in the Allied command, on December 20, 1944, he was promoted to General of the Army, equivalent to rank of Field Marshall in most European armies. In this and the previous high commands he held, Eisenhower showed his great talents for leadership and diplomacy. Although he had never seen action himself, he won the respect of front-line commanders. He dealt skillfully with difficult subordinates such as Omar Bradley and Patton, and allies such as Winston Churchill, Field Marshall Bernard Montgomery and General Charles De Gaulle. He negotiated with Soviet Marshal Zhukov and sometimes worked directly with Stalin.

Following the unconditional surrender on 8 May 1945, Eisenhower was appointed Military Governor of the occupied force based in Frankfurt am Main.

Nazi Germany was divided into four occupation zones, one each for the U.S., Britain, France, and the Soviet Union. Upon full discovery of the death camps that were part of the final solution (Holocaust), he ordered camera crews to comprehensively document evidence of the atrocity for use in the war crimes tribunals.

He made the decision to reclassify German prisoners of war (POWs) in U.S. custody as Disarmed Enemy Forces (DEFs), thus depriving them of the protection of the Geneva Convention. As DEFs, their food rations could be lowered and they could be compelled to serve as free labor.

Eisenhower was an early supporter of the Morgenthau Plan to permanently remove Germany's industrial capacity to wage future wars, in which over one- million German (DEF's) might die of harsh conditions.

In November 1945, he approved the distribution of 1000 free copies of Henry Morgenthau Junior's book, *Germany is Our Problem*, which promoted and described the plan in detail, to American military officials in occupied Germany. Historian Stephen Ambrose draws the conclusion that, despite Eisenhower's later claims the act was not an endorsement of the Morgenthau plan, Eisenhower both approved of the plan and had previously given Morgenthau at least some of his ideas about how Germany should be treated.

He also incorporated officials from Morgenthau's Treasury Department into the army of occupation. These were commonly called "Morgenthau boys" for their zeal in interpreting the occupation directive JCS 1067, which had been heavily influenced by Morgenthau and his plan as strictly as possible.

Eisenhower served as Chief of Staff of the United States Army from 1945-48. In December 1950, he was named Supreme Commander of the North Atlantic Treaty Organization (NATO), and given operational command of NATO forces in Europe. Eisenhower retired from active service on 31 May 1952.

Upon entering politics, he wrote "Crusade in Europe", widely regarded as one of the finest U.S. military memoirs. During this period Eisenhower served as President of Columbia University from 1948 until 1953, though he was on leave from the university while he served as NATO commander.

General of the Army, Dwight D. Eisenhower, Chief of Staff of the United States Army. After his many wartime successes, General Eisenhower returned to the U.S. a great hero. He was unusual for a military hero as he never saw the front line in his life.

The nearest he came to being under enemy fire was in 1944 when a German fighter strafed the ground while he was inspecting troops in Normandy. Eisenhower dived for cover like everyone else and after the plane flew off, a British brigadier helped him up and seemed very relieved he was not hurt. When Eisenhower thanked him for his solicitude, the brigadier deflated him by explaining "my concern was that you should not be injured in my sector." This incident formed part of Eisenhower's fund of stories he would tell now and again.

Not long after his return, a "Draft Eisenhower" movement in the Republican Party persuaded him to declare his candidacy in the 1952 presidential election, in order to counter the candidacy of non-interventionist of Senator Robert A. Taft. Eisenhower had been courted by both parties in 1948 and had declined to run then. Eisenhower defeated Taft for the nomination but came to an agreement that Taft would stay out of foreign affairs while Eisenhower followed a conservative domestic policy.

Eisenhower's campaign was a crusade against the Truman administration's policies regarding "Korea, Communism and

Corruption" and was also noted for the simple but effective phrase "I Like Ike." Eisenhower promised to go to Korea himself and end the war and maintains both a strong NATO opposition abroad against communism and a corruption-free frugal administration at home.

He and his running mate Richard Nixon, whose daughter later married Eisenhower's grandson David, defeated Democrat Adlai Stevenson.

Eisenhower was the only general to serve as President in the twentieth century, and the most recent President, until the inauguration of Donald Trump in 2017, to have never held elected office prior to the Presidency. (The other Presidents not to have held prior elected office were Zachary Taylor, Ulysses S. Grant, William Taft, and Herbert Hoover.)

President Eisenhower was the United States President from 20 January 1953 – 20 January 1961.

In his farewell address to the nation Eisenhower expressed his concerns about the dangers of massive military spending, particularly deficit spending and government contracts to private military manufacturers. Evaluations of his presidency place him among the upper tier of U.S. Presidents.

Nuremberg Trials: The truth of the matter is that the fact that a defendant had acted under an order of his government or of a superior was not to free him of responsibility for having carried it out. With the trials coming up the regulations were changed to provide that an order that offended a soldier's conscience need not be carried out.

The leaders of the Nazi Party after the war were tried in Nuremberg, Germany. The Tribunal was made up of four members and four alternates; two judges from each of the Allied Powers. The courtroom holding approximately 600 people was held on the second floor of the Palace of Justice. Every seat in the courtroom was occupied except the twenty-one chairs reserved for, the accused.

At mid-night, on 15-16 October 1945, the Palace of Justice where the prisoners were staffed, in the center of Nuremberg, was deathlike silent as the war criminals laid in their beds listening to the bells of the cathedral tower ringing out for the last time.

They had heard those bells many times before during celebrations and ceremonies, when the Fuhrer would be gloating about his power to the citizens of Germany. And during that time the city district was beautiful and historic at that same location. Now all that remained was a prison, a scattering of destroyed houses, the bell tower of the cathedral, a pyramid of rubbish against fallen buildings, destroyed by the Allied armies on 7 January 1945.

Many of the Germans that lived through the war and survived said that they were ignorant of what went on during the war years. This I do not believe, with all the freight cars of dead bodies on railroad sidings. It is a terrible page in our history of the human race.

In Germany the citizens that prevailed cared less about the war criminals that had destroyed their livelihood and Germany in twelve years, and now that it's destroyed, just the busy traffic of the Allied countries officials and the American occupation remained. The Council of Ministers for the trials that were addressed was to prove the criminals were guilty was also taking place so that the citizens of Germany would realize that their conquerors not only destroyed their country they also destroyed Germany's great works of music, science, literature, philosophy and scholarships that had been of creative achievements, now smashed.

At the end of World War Two the United States held trials for about three-hundred war criminals. The criminals that were tried were the organizers of the crimes, the leaders in high command in the Nazi Party and the State, and the Army, Navy, the diplomats, bankers, judges, bureaucrats, and industrialist. To name a few, Hitler, Goering, Hess, Ribbentrop, Goebbels, Himmler and Rosenberg were all main creators.

Let it be known that a defendant that acted under order of his superior was not to free him of responsibility for carrying out the order. It is documented in the official regulations that no order that would offend the soldiers conscience or improper conduct need not to be carried out. Between the period of July 1945 and July 1949, one-hundred-ninety-nine people were tried, thirty-eight were acquitted, thirty-six sentenced to death, eighteen were executed, twenty-three to life imprisonment and one-hundred-eighty-four- twenty to death.

Presiding over the trials was Lord Justice Lawrence, with endured patience during all the proceedings. The Versailles Treaty on any German politics and discussions was not allowed during the Nuremberg trials. The documents for the trials for the SS alone filled six freight cars. When Justice Jackson reported to President Truman, he said that there were six million pages of typewritten record.

THE TRIALS – Martin Bormann, was the second in command of Hitler's deputies. He was in charge of the party's Aid Fund, making himself a new career in the National Socialism Organization, before the appointment Bormann worked as a farm hand.

In 1929 he married Greta Bach, they had ten children, the first was named Adolf, Hitler attended the wedding. In 1946, Bormann's wife died in Italy from cancer. Bormann was not present at the trials, his where about was not known. Rumor had it that he escaped to Argentina or Brazil. Bormann's crimes consisted of more crimes than the court could count. And so the defense condemned Bormann to death, simply on the account that he was still alive. No statute of limitations exists for Bormann dead or alive.

Karl Doenitz, who commanded the German submarines of the Navy during World War Two, was first their Chief and then as Commander in Chief of the Navy. As a submarine officer his attention on the U-boats rather than the Navy strategy led Raeder to oppose Doenitz succeeding him in 1944; Hitler overruled the objection. Admiral Doenitz along with Admiral Raeder was charged with the most despicable crimes carried out by naval officers, not only was they accused of plotting to wage aggressive warfare and then waged it. They had made no effort to rescue the survivors of torpedoed ships, but instead had ordered the survivors to be shot as they lay in boats or floated in the water. The prosecution also charged the two Naval Officers that sent to their deaths hundreds of noncombatants, including women and children that had been passengers on merchant ships. For his crimes the Tribunal sentenced him to ten years in prison, Doenitz spent ten years and twenty days before he was released.

Hans Frank, was an ambitious attorney and a success in the National Socialist Party, he had been chief legal authority of the Party almost since he received his law degree in 1926. By the time 1943 rolled around, Germany was doing well with its aggression war on all the smaller countries. Frank was now serving as Governor General; he was a world figure with his own palace and his own railroad car, and the only one with the title in all the Reich. He ruled with an iron hand, except for the police. Like the Fuhrer, he had a deputy, a higher SS and police leader and many departments, the interior, justice, education, construction, and propaganda.

In a meeting in December 1941, Frank told the soldiers at a meeting that as far as the Jews were concerned, I want to tell you quite frankly that they must be done away with in one way or another, in December 1942. Eighty-five percent of the Jews of the General Government had been transported to extermination centers. Frank had known from the beginning the extermination of the Jews and he approved it.

Wilhelm Frick was the Minister of the Interior, during the trials he failed to take the stand. He was head of the political section of the Munich Police Department, until 1923, when he took over the Criminal section. Frick drafted the basic laws under which other bureaucrats could operate the National Socialist State, with the conscience that everything they did was legal. Frick could issue a decree in effect placing Jews outside the law and turn them over to the Gestapo. At the Nuremberg trials the estimated people put to death was around 275,000, including 75,000 old people a later calculation estimated between 70,000 and 80,000. Frick was a participant in these killings, he did not delight in them but felt it necessary as he thought the laws he signed giving the sole power for the police and guards at the concentration and extermination camps were necessary. The court at the trials found him guilty of every charge except having waged-aggressive war and sentenced him to death.

Hans Fritzsche, he was the propagandist, Chief of German broadcasting, he was sentenced for nine years. Fritzsche was freed in time to live a couple of years with his second wife; he died of cancer in 1953.

Walter Emanuel Funk, the man who succeeded Schacht as Minister of Economics in 1938, was the final cause of Schacht's dismissal in 1939 as president of the Reichsbank. Funk, of self-style free enterprise, who joined the party in order to preserve the market economy. German businessmen believed in therapeutic doses of government intervention and in well-deposited government to support them.

At the Nuremberg trials Funk admitted that he placed the will of the state against his own conscience and sense of duty, to this he pleaded guilty. The court found him guilty of waging aggressive warfare and of having committed war crimes and crimes against humanity. The court admitted that Funk was never a dominate figure and it was this that saved him from being hung. He was sentenced to life imprisonment. Funk was released from prison in 1957 because of ill health, three years later he died.

Hermann Goring, he was charged with: four counts waged aggressive warfare, he had plotted it, he had committed war crimes, and he had committed crimes against humanity. The mass murder of 11,000 polish soldiers in the Katyn Forest, was the work of the Nazi Conspirators, Goring was one of them. After his long gruesome trial Goring was charged guilty and scheduled to be hung. Unfortunately he did not get the hang-mans-noose because someone smuggled him a cyanide capsule and he died.

Rudolf Hess, when Hitler became Reich Chancellor, Hess became third man in the Reich; he was the Fuhrer's private secretary and attendant. In June of 1920, he was head of the National Socialist Party at the University. He was arrested in 1923, when he took part in the Beer Hall Putsch with the Fuhrer, and served time with him for eighteen months. When World War Two began, Hess wanted to fly for the Reich, because he was a pilot in World War One, but Hitler ordered him to stay at his post.

When Hess overheard Hitler saying that he could not understand why the British were fighting a war they could not win; Hess took it upon himself to get hold of a private airplane and secretly fly to England, because he wanted England to sign a peace agreement with Germany to please his leader. He landed in Scotland, when he landed, he was in a Nazi uniform and was arrested, when he was searched, they found drugs on him and arrested him. They soon found out that the drugs were for Hess's drug addiction. Hess explained to them the secret of his journey and that he wanted to talk to the Duke of Hamilton so he would put him in touch with the King and the Peace Party. In Hess's psychotic mind he pictured himself as a savior and peace maker. After discussing the reason for his visit and that Hitler did not know he was there, but that Hitler did want peace with the British.

Hess wanted to be back in Germany in a few days, with an offer from the King of England for a peace agreement, apparently he was out of touch from reality, for neither the British nor Germans were pleased with him. Churchill did not want it known that a third party from Germany had come to make a peace offering, and that a Peace Party in Britain did not exist. Churchill ordered that Hess be considered a prisoner of war, isolated and well treated. Hess stayed in the British prison until the end of the war and then was taken to Germany to be charged as a war criminal and held for trial.

The Tribunal in Nuremberg believed that Hess state of mind was in poor condition, "hysterical amnesia", his attorney said that Hess was manifestly abnormal, consequently he was allowed to testify on his own behalf, but he never did so. Hess was found quality of conspiring to wage warfare and of having waged it, also of planning attacks on Poland, Norway, Yugoslavia, the Low Countries and the others, including the Soviet Union, and there was knowledge of him being insane when he committed these crimes against them. He was sentenced to life in prison.

Alfred Jodl, Jodl had fought in World War One, and had thought of studying medicine, after the war, but decided to stay in the Army, his superiors thought well of him, an eager and excellent leader, and suitable for higher command. From 1935 to 1938, he was Chief of National Defense section of the Wehrmachtsamt (the principal administrative agency within the OKW). In 1940, he became General of Artillery and Colonel General in 1944. After a lengthy trial in Nuremberg, Jodl was found guilty and sentenced death.

Ernst Kaltenbrunner, after 1943 he headed up the RSHA, the Reich Security Main Office, with the rank of General to the police. Under RSHA was the Secret Police of the Reich with the authority of the concentration and the extermination camps. Ernst was charged with three counts, war crimes, and crimes against humanity.

Wilhelm Keitel, he was a soldier in Hitler's army of high caliber. Keitel order that every village in which partisan was found must be burned down and victims suspected of offenses against the German troops shot without trial. Keitel was found guilty and sentenced to hang, he pleaded with the court to be shot, rather than be hung, and he was denied.

Constantin Von Neurath, was charged with all four counts and sentenced to fifteen years in prison, of which, he was released after serving eight years. Neurath was in bad physical condition at the age of eighty-one years. He passed away in 1956.

Franz Von Papen, was found not guilty by the Tribunal, he was released and then captured again and arrested by the German authorities in Wuerttemberg and Bavaria, charging him as a major offender. Two German courts found him guilty, the first sentenced him to eight years in prison, the second court placed him in a lesser category of offences and freed him with a charge of 30,000 marks, of which was to be given as contribution to the restitution funds given people who had suffered under the Nazis.

Erich Raeder, was a Navy Chief, after meeting with the Fuehrer in 1933, he considered Hitler as being a greatly gifted man, endowed with charisma so powerful that Raeder sought to avoid personal meetings. Because of the Fuhrer's ability to convince people of the soundness of his views against their will and better judgment, he kept away from which may be occasions when he might be alone with Hitler.

Raeder was convicted of planning and waging warfare, the main charge against Raeder is that he had committed war crimes. For his method of committing submarine warfare, that included the sinking of the Athena. The last and most serious charge against him was the carrying out of the so-called Commando Order.

For his crimes, the court sentenced him to life imprisonment; he was seventy years old at the time and was released ten years later for good behavior.

Alfred Rosenberg, after Rosenberg was captured and pulled off to prison the American soldiers found his diary hidden in a Castle where he was hiding. Rosenberg was the Chief Visionary of the party, anti-church, anti-Semitic, anti-Slav.

Because he was a writer, and a voluminous writer, he had written several books. Little was left out of the part that he played in the National Socialist Party. Rosenberg's position was to confiscate Jewish and Masonic property.

Between the period of October 1940 and July 1944, he had recorded and taken as ownership of Jewish property 21,903 art objects of all kind ship to the Reich in twenty-nine shipments, including 39 freight trains. There were paintings by Rembrandt, Rubens, Velasquez, Murillo, Goya, Boucher, Watteau, Cranach, and Reynolds. Plus, 681 miniatures, 583 textiles, goblins', rugs, embroideries, bronzes, vases, and a collection of French furniture. This was all recorded on activities of the Einsatzstab Rosenberg. The courts found him guilty of all counts and sentenced him to hang.

Fritz Sauckel, from the end of March until the end of the war Sauckel worked as head of the forced-labor program, he did his work efficiently and tirelessly as he organized millions of people. At the Nuremberg trials he was found as committing crimes against humanity and war crimes, he was sentenced to be hanged.

Hjalmar Schacht, was among the most prominent. The prosecution called him the wizard and respectable front for the hoodlums who clubbed the opposition off the streets. In the Nuremberg trials Schacht was acquitted. Although the Russians voted for finding him guilty, and Justice Jackson found his acquittal regrettable, the United States classifications officer for that state said the decision was incomprehensible. Nevertheless he was freed and was able to start a new life for himself.

Baldur Von Schirach, was the Youth Leader, the court found him guilty of committing crimes against humanity and sentenced him to twenty years in prison.

Arthur Seyss-Inquart, a Deputy Governor of Frank's in Poland. Arthur Seyss-Inquart walked with a limp, he had a bald spot atop of his head that was concealed by the way he combed his hair, and wore thick reading glasses, he was an inspiring young attorney during World War Two, at the Nuremberg trials he was one of the youngest at fifty-four years old. He was born in 1892, in the town of Iglau in Moravia on the border of Slav. At the age of fifteen his family moved to Vienna, where he studied law at the university. In 1914 he enlisted in the Austro Hungarian Army where he fought on the Russian and Italian fronts, during a furlough he received his law degree.

Arthur became a member of the German Brotherhood that was to liberate the German people from Jewish authority, it was a secret organization.

The courts found Seyss-Inquart guilty of three of the four counts, he planned to wage war, he had waged it and he had committed crimes against humanity.

Albert Speer, when Speer was only thirty-six years old he became Minister of Arms and Munitions, he was an architect by occupation. He was put in the position of the production of armaments, during his ministry he kept up with production until the period of 1945.

The Tribunal found Speer guilty of war crimes and crimes against humanity. He was not found guilty of planning or waging war. He was sentenced for twenty years.

Julius Streicher, stayed true to the Fuhrer until the end, Streicher was a writer of source, and had written many publications on the disposal of the Jews, because he believed as did Hitler that they were the cause of the Germans losing the First World War. He told the Nuremberg people on 3 April 1925, "that for thousands of years the Jews have been destroying the German people and the rest of the world; and make it the beginning today that we can destroy the Jew". Streicher was sentenced to hang, his last words on the gallows were: Heil Hitler".

After the executions the bodies of each man was placed in a wooden box/coffin. A tag bearing the name of each deceased was pinned on their garments. With the hangman's noose still around his neck, each man was photographed. The body of Goring was brought in and placed upon its box to be photographed with the others. In the early morning hours, two trucks carrying eleven caskets left the prison compound at the Palace of Justice bound for crematories at Dachau Concentration Camp near Munich, where eleven corpses were burned to ashes. It was reported that evening the eleven urns containing the ashes were taken away to be emptied into the river Isar in West Germany.

The defendants who had received sentences of imprisonment were transferred to Span Day Prison. As years passed the defendants completed their terms and released. The last prisoner was Rudolf Hess, who had been sentenced for life. On 17 August 1987, forty-one years after the final judgment of the Tribunal, Hess managed to commit suicide. With his death, Hitler's tyranny ended.

Japanese War Crimes Trials

In 1946, Tokyo, Japan, the International Military Tribunals for the Far East began hearings of twenty-eight Japanese military and government officials accused of committing war crimes and crimes against humanity during World War Two.

On 4 November 1948, the trials ended with twenty-five of twenty-eight Japanese defendants being found guilty. Of the three other defendants, two had died during the lengthy trial, and one was declared insane. On 12 November, the War Crimes Tribunal passed death sentences on seven of the men, including General Hideki Tojo, who served as Japanese premier during the war, and other principals, such as Iwane Matsui, who organized the Rape of Nanking, and Heitaro Kimura, who brutalized Allied prisoners of war. Sixteen others were sentenced to life imprisonment, and two were sentenced to lesser terms in prison. On 23 December 1948 Tojo and the six others were executed in Tokyo.

Unlike the Nuremberg trial of Nazi war criminals, where there were four chief prosecutors, to represent Great Britain, France, the United States, and the USSR, the Tokyo trial featured only one chief prosecutor-American Joseph B. Keenan, a former assistant to the U. S. Attorney General. However, other nations, especially China, contributed to the proceedings, and Australian Judge William Flood Webb presided. In addition to the central Tokyo trial, various Tribunals sitting outside Japan judged some 5,000 Japanese guilty of war crimes, of whom more than 900 were executed. Some observers thought that Emperor Hirohito should have been tried for his tacit approval of Japanese policy during the war, but he was protected by U.S. authorities who saw him as a symbol of Japanese unity and conservatism, both favorable trials in the postwar United States view.

Japanese, POWs in the Pacific Theater capacity, thirty-four percent American, thirty-three percent Australian, thirty-two percent British, the rest were assorted countries.

CHAPTER NINE

"DO YOU KNOW"

President Roosevelt and Adolf Hitler died eighteen days of each other – Roosevelt had a massive heart stroke while sitting for his portrait, looking forward to an international conference that would charter the United States. Hitler shot himself in the head.

FDR's code name was "Victor"

The largest amount of aircraft produced during World War II was the Messerschmitt BF-109E with nearly 36,000 produced.

Joe E. Brown was the most traveled entertainer during World War II. He traveled approximately 150, 000 miles.

The first USAAF aircraft to see action on 4 July 1942 was the Douglas A-20G Havoc.

There were thirteen 50-caliber machine guns aboard the B-17 Flying Fortress.

The largest production of tanks produced during the war was the Sherman Tank, for a total of 49,000 units. Russia produced 40,000 T34/76 tanks, for the #2 position.

Japan produced approximately 65,000 aircraft during the war, 9,000 were left at the end of the war.

At the Normandy Invasion the British with twelve minesweepers cleared the waters close to the French shore at night on the 5th of June 1944.

The American aircraft industry in 1944 produced one plane every six minutes.

A tradition among most of the world's largest armies was exchange trainee programs – until the war started in 1938. General Albert Wedemeyer returned to the U. S. after spending two years as an exchange trainee at the German War College, the Kriegsakademie, in Berlin. He reported to the chief of staff in United States when he returned, on what he had seen as an aggressive growth of military in Germany. "No one was interested".

Between 1939 and 1945 Germany sunk 2,800 Allied ships with U-boats.

When the German Battleship Bismarck was sunk, it was carrying two-thousand plus Navy crew members aboard; only one-thousand-ten were rescued by the British.

At the time of Pearl Harbor the top U. S. Navy command was called CINCUS, (Commander –in- Chief US), (pronounced "sink us").

The shoulder patch of the U. S. Army's 45th Infantry Division was the Swastika.

And Hitler's private train was named "Amerika". All three were soon changed for PR purpose, when the United States entered into World War Two.

A blue star hung in windows of families during the war that had sons in the military, a gold star would hang in the window when one was killed.

German prisoners of war were delivered by the Axis and sent to Georgia in September 1943, to pick peanuts (about 130,000 prisoners). Also 400 Italian prisoners were sent to Charleston, South Carolina to work at the Fertilizer Plant.

Arlington National Cemetery

Outside of Washington D.C. lays a cemetery, it is a military cemetery for American veterans, and its name is called Arlington National Cemetery, and is located in Arlington, Virginia. It is the burial ground for more than 400,000 military service members, veterans and family members. The cemetery contains several memorials including the Tomb of the Unknown Soldier, a monument dedicated to United States service members whose remains were never identified. The cemetery is guarded day and night by Marine Guards.

CHAPTER TEN

THE KOREAN WAR

On the 12th day of March 1947, President Truman opened a meeting with Congress, stating the following message.

One of the primary objects of the foreign policy of the United States is the creation of conditions in which we and other nations will be able to work out a way of life free from coercion... We shall not realize our objectives, however, unless we are willing to help free peoples to maintain their free institutions and their national integrity against aggressive movements that seek to impose upon them totalitarian regimes.

This is no more than a recognition that totalitarian regimes imposed upon free peoples, by direct or indirect aggression, undermine the foundations of international peace and hence the security of the United States.

On 25 June 1950, South Koreans were awoken by a divine nightmare; unexpected and unannounced the war in Korea begins. President Truman was in the White House. General MacArthur was appointed Supreme Commander of the United States, and Chief of Command to assist the South Koreans.

In July 1950, the first American troops arrived in South Korea as part of the United Nations effort to support the South Koreans. The United States troop's first impression of Korea came through their nostrils. Korea was literally a stinking place. GI's got a whiff of Kimchi fermenting cabbage, buried along roadsides. But the aroma was very tame compared with the stench that came from honey wagons, which were ox-pulled carts of human excrement that fertilized Korean rice patties. And the American troops had difficulty in distinguishing between the North and South Koreans or any other Asians.

Korea terrain is a difficult frontier to travel on; it is not easy for an army to launch an attack. So it is difficult to figure out why with approximately five-hundred U. S. Officers and nearly seven-hundred noncombatants technical support occupying South Korea, the Armed forces were unable to detect the build-up of the North Korean forces while it was taking place. Also, the South Koreans had ships in the harbor ready to evacuate the families of the American officers, and other South Koreans, the question remains as to whether the attack was purely a surprise.

The initial attack force consisted of four divisions, assisted by three military units, arranged along the four different front locations at the 38th parallel. There were also seventy tanks; the force total was approximately seventy-thousand men.

Seventy years later, still is the unanswered question of who wanted the war? Some express that it was the soybean market. Investigations found that a large group of Chinese names in this country and in Hong Kong were holders of open contracts of the commodity. Also, was the close connection between South Korean President Syngman Rhee and Chian Kai shek government in Formosa.

The Potsdam Conference was held at Cecilienhof, the home of Crown Prince Wilhelm in Potsdam, occupied Germany, from 17 July to 2 August 1945. The participants were the United States, Truman, The United Kingdom, Churchill, and the Soviet Union, Stalin.

At the conference decisions were made that would affect countries around the world. Korea was divided at the 38th Parallel, the North and South. The decision made was to have the United States troops occupy the South Koreans, and that the Soviet Union occupying the North Koreans.

In 1948 pre-elections were held and supervised at the United Nations, however only the South Koreans voted, the Soviet Union forbid the voting of North Korea, the area under it.

In North Korea, a socialist state under the communist leadership of Kim Il-sung, and a capitalist state in South Korea lead by President Syngman Rhee.

Events in Asia also contributed to an increased sense of insecurity. In 1949 China underwent a revolution that brought Mao Zedong and his Communist party into power. The nationalists, led by Chiang Kai-Shek, had retreated to the island of Formosa (Taiwan) while they continued their war with mainland China. Mao quickly moved to ally himself with the Soviet Union, and signed a treaty with the Soviets in 1950. The Truman administration faced criticism from Republicans who claimed he had "lost" China. They criticized him for not providing enough aid to the Chinese nationalists. The suggestion by Secretary of State Dean Acheson that the administration recognize the communist government of China only gave them more ammunition for the attacks.

The Truman administration also faced internal criticism regarding its commitment to anticommunism at home. Republican Senator Joseph McCarthy of Wisconsin had recently begun his infamous hunt for communists within the U. S. Government. Although McCarthy was just warming up, the recent trial of Alger Hiss and others for espionage left the Truman administration apprehensive about its anticommunist's credentials. Truman and his advisors found themselves under increased domestic pressure not to appear "soft" on communism abroad.

When the Korean invasion took place, the Truman Administration seized upon the opportunity to defend a noncommunist government from invasion by communist troops. Determined not to "lose" another country to communism, and interested in shoring up its anticommunist credentials the Truman administration found itself defending a nation a world away from U. S. soil. Yet Truman's response was not merely a response to internal pressure. The invasion of South Korea made Truman genuinely fearful that the Soviet Union and China intended to expand the sphere of communism throughout Asia.

The invasion escalated into combat when North Korean forces crossed the border (38 Parallel), and advanced into South Korea. The security council of the United Nations authorized the dispatch of forces to Korea. Eventually, there were twenty-one countries that answered the call. The United States provided approximately ninety percent of the military personnel.

On 25 October, China entered the war in support of the North; they were outnumbered and outgunned.

On the Pacific Coast one of the Navy Escort Carriers was taken out of moth balls and made ready for an American fleet and supported by a British fleet as they streamed toward Korea to patrol the Coast. Army troops went ashore at Pusan, port of entry on the South East Coast of Korea; the men were drawn from the 8th Army, an Army of occupation in Japan. General Walker and the 24th Division constantly tried to fill the gaps in a long thin line.

The first objective of the invaders was to take Seoul, the capital city, and they did, the country was overrun, except for a small pocket around the Port of Pusan.

At the Pusan Perimeter United Nations forces had to cling to a toehold that was hardly more than an expanded beachhead in order to defend the strip of land at the lowest end of the peninsula protecting the only port and airfield the Americans had left where they could land reinforcements and supplies.

At the beginning of August, Maj. Gen. Walton Walker said in a desperate bid to rally his troops, we must fight to the end; we must fight as a team. If some of us die, we will die fighting together. The result at the Pusan port ended up being the greatest butcheries in history.

The Americans had some advantage; they controlled the sea and skies, which prohibited the North Koreans from moving in day-light if they wanted to escape jet fighters and naval batteries.

By August of 1950, U. S. troops had been pinned down at the southeast corner of the Korean peninsula called the Pusan Perimeter. There was no place left to go on the Korean peninsula as the only thing behind them was the sea. The solution from General Douglas MacArthur headquarters was to stage an invasion at Inchon, a maneuver to draw the attention away from the point of action.

Inchon was also only twenty miles from the South Korean capital of Seoul, which had been occupied by North Korean troops. General MacArthur intended to open a second front behind the North Koreans. A seaborne assault launched upon the Port of Inchon on 15 September was later documented as one of the most significant operations of the Korean War.

The Inchon invasion was by far one of the most daring and risky amphibious operations conducted by the U. S. Navy. The steep rocky shores and 30-foot tides in the harbor made the task seem impossible. Task Force 7, consisting of over 200 ships and United Nations forces succeeded in taking Inchon. United Nations troops quickly moved inland behind the overextended North Korean advance, and cut its line of supply. These forces lead the recapture of Seoul and eased the pressure on U.S. troops trapped at Pusan. As the U. S. forces advanced, they pushed the North Koreans back across the 38th Parallel.

The ground troops were continually sent out on patrols to try and find the enemy, and determine or try to find out what they were up to. Sometimes, patrols would scout beyond the 38th Parallel at night when it would be difficult to be seen by the enemy.

Commonly used squad-level weapons included the fully-automatic M2 carbine (a small rifle) and the M1911 45 caliber pistol. Conditions in the trenches or dug-outs alongside of hills were very bleak, indeed. In the field, it was very cold, fifteen and twenty degrees above zero, and below zero at times during the winter months. The troops could hear sounds of artillery hitting the trenches and even though they could not see the enemy, they would return rounds.

The phosphorous flares that the enemy used created extremely troublesome casualties. The flares would burst with an extremely bright white light, and the burning phosphorous would cling to the soldiers and burn them. The only way that medics could extinguish the burning phosphorous or get it off was to apply mud packs to the wounds. The veterans told me it was awful hearing their comrades scream while the phosphorous was burning on them. The other veterans kept busy making mud packs.

The Chosen-Reservoir-between 27 November and around the middle of December 1950; the day after Thanksgiving the United Nation troops were getting into position around the Chosen Reservoir, the freezing point was dropping steadily. It was about twenty degrees below freezing, and everything was turning to ice.

A notorious seventeen day and night battle followed between about 30,000 United Nations troops and the 67,000 Chinese troops that had surrounded the U. N. troops at the Chosen Reservoir. After days and nights of cold and brutal fighting, the Marines formed into a convoy with a single M4A3 Sherman tank at the front.

On 1 December, the 3rd Battalion, 7th Marines engaged the PVA 175th, Regiment of the 59th Division, at Hill 1542 and Hill 1419, unfortunately the Chinese garrison drove the Marines back and they had to dig in on the icy slopes.

Besides the troops on Hill 1542 and 1419, there were on the other three sides of the entrapment United Nation troops trying to break through. Although the Chinese troops outnumbered the UN forces, the United Nation forces broke out of the siege. The evacuation of the X-Corps from the port of Hungnam marked the complete withdrawal of UN troops from the North Koreans at the Frozen Chosen, December 1950.

Fifteen Congressional Medals of Honor were awarded to individual troops that fought at the Chosen reservoir campaign.

The Korean War ultimately involved twenty-two countries and left Korea a smoking ruin that stank of death. More than four-million men, women and children were killed, wounded or otherwise incapacitated in the war, including two million civilians in North and South Korea. Truman's police action?, no, in my own opinion the Korean War was not a police action, when you have two countries or two sides of a country fighting and killing each other, hey Congress, "that is a war". The Korean War left 54,246 Americans dead, including 33,629 in combat and 20,617 killed from accidents or illness. There were also 103,284 Americans wounded.

Taking advantage of the UN Command's strategic momentum against the communists, General MacArthur believed it necessary to extend the Korean War into China to destroy depots supplying the North Korean war effort. President Truman disagreed, and ordered caution at the Sino-Korean border.

General MacArthur crossed the 38th Parallel in a belief that the Chinese would not enter the war. Because of this there were major allied losses. He believed that whether to use nuclear weapons should be his decision, and not the presidents. MacArthur threatened to destroy China unless it surrendered.

Because of these actions, President Truman on 11 April 1951 told General MacArthur that he was relieved as being the Supreme Commander in Korea.

Because he defied the orders of the president, which is a violation of the U. S. Constitution, in May and June MacArthur was the subject of congressional hearings. The main reason that President Truman did not want the Allied forces crossing into China is that it would provoke the Soviet Union into entering the war.

General Ridgeway was appointed Supreme Commander in Korea; replacing General MacArthur, he regrouped the UN forces for successful counterattacks. For the remainder of the war the United Nations and the PVA/KPA fought but exchanged little territory, as the stalemate held.

Large-scale bombing of North Korea continued, and protracted armistice negotiations began on 10 July 1951 at Kaesong, an ancient capital of North Korea located in PVA/KPA held territory. Combat continued while the belligerents negotiated; the goal of the UN forces was to recapture all of South Korea and to avoid losing territory. From December 1951 to March 1952, Republic of Korea (ROK) security forces claimed to have killed 11,090 partisans and sympathizers and captured 9,916 more.

With peace negotiations ongoing, the Chinese attempted one final offensive in the final weeks of the year to capture territory. On 10 June, 30,000 Chinese troops struck two South Korean and one U. S. division on an eight-mile front, and on 13 July, they struck the east-central Kumsong sector. In both cases, the Chinese had some success in penetrating South Korean lines, but failed to capitalize.

The United States in 1952 elected a new president, Dwight D. Eisenhower, in November of 1952, the president-elect went to Korea to learn what might end the Korean War.

The Korean People's Army (KPA) and the People's Volunteer Army (PVA) and the United Nation (UN) Command signed the Korean Armistice Agreement on 27 July 1953; South Korean President Syngman Rhee refused to sign the agreement. The war is considered to have ended at this point, even though there was no peace treaty. North Korea nevertheless claims that it won the Korean War.

After the war, Operation Glory was conducted from July to November 1954, to allow combatant countries to exchange their dead. The remains of 4,167 US Army and US Marine Corps dead were exchanged for 13,528 KPA and PVA dead, and 546 civilians that died in UN prisoner-of-war camps were delivered to the South Korea government.

As far as I know there has not been any action since 27 April 2018, when it was announced that North Korea and South Korea agreed to talks to end the ongoing 65-year war. They committed to the complete denuclearization of the Korean Peninsula.

Major General John H. Church: For my featured warrior during the Korean War, I have chosen Major General Church. During the opening days of the Korean War, Church provided assistance to the South Korean Army; he was there in the opening days of the war. He later commanded the 24th Infantry Division while it was engaged in the Battle of the Pusan Perimeter.

John Huston Church was born in the town of Glen Iron in Pennsylvania on 28 June 1892. From 1915 until 1917, he was a student of New York University. When the United States entered into World War One, Church volunteered into the U. S. Army and was commissioned as a second lieutenant.

Church served with the 28th Infantry Regiment on the Western Front as part of the 1st Division of the American Expeditionary Force. He was wounded twice and was awarded a Distinguished Service Cross for heroism in action at the Battle of Cantigny.

After WWI, Church decided to stay in the service and was aide-de-camp to Brigadier Gen. F. C. Marshall in 1920. After being promoted to captain, he served at post as an instructor with the National Guard in Maryland.

In October 1945, Church became the assistant chief of staff for operations of the 45th Infantry Division. When the United States entered World War II, Church was appointed Chief of Staff for the 45th Infantry Division, and served with the division until late 1943. Following that he became Assistant Division Commander during which time he was involved in the Allied invasion of Sicily. He fought in numerous battles in the Italian Campaign and Operation Dragoon, then in the Allied Invasion of Southern France. From 1943 to mid-1944 Church held regimental command when he led the 57th Infantry Regiment.

In September of 1944, Church was promoted to the one-star General officer rank of Brigadier General and posted to the 84th Infantry Division as its ADC. He was wounded again when his division took part in the advance from the Netherlands to the Elbe River towards the end of the war.

After the war, Church became the commander of the Infantry Replacement Training Center at Fort McClellan, Alabama. He was given the same post at Fort Jackson, South Carolina. From 1948 until 1949 Church served as deputy chief of Army Field Forces at Fort Monroe, Virginia. In 1950, he was serving in General Douglas MacArthur's headquarters in Tokyo as a section chief.

When the war broke out in Korea, MacArthur sent Church to lead a survey team of staff officers to work with Ambassador Muccio and the Korean Military Advisory Group, and assess what assistance could be provided to the South Korean Army.

The first army unit sent over from Japan was under the command of Major General William F. Dean. A reinforced company of the division, commanded by Lieutenant Colonel Brad Smith, was sent north from Pusan to try to halt the North Koreans. Meeting at Taejon, Church informed him "All we need is some men up there who won't run when they see tanks", and instructed Smith to make his stand at Osan. Smith was without tank support and had faulty communications, and was promptly overrun in its first engagement with the North Koreans. Dean gathered his troops in the city of Taejon and formed a strong defense. After a stubborn fight, the American troops retreated. Dean got separated from his troops and was captured. On 22 July, Church, without a command following the dissolution of ADCOM, was given command of the division.

After a two day rest period, Lieutenant General Walton Walker, the commander of the U. S. Eighth Army, decided that he needed the 24th to guard the Southwest line (the Naktong Bulge) of the Pusan Perimeter. During the subsequent battle, the North Korean 6th Division inflicted more losses on Church's men and gradually pushed the 24th back. Finally, Church by now promoted to Major General, was able to regroup his men and they held the perimeter, especially with the help of a brigade of marines.

Suffering from arthritis, General Church remained in command of the 24th until 25 January 1951. His health meant that he was not often in the field and Lieutenant Gen. Matthew Ridgway, commander of the U. S. Eighth Army following the death of Walker in December 1950, considered this was detrimental to the state of the division. Ridgway relieved Church of his command, and replaced him with Brigadier General Blackshear M. Bryan. General Church was awarded the Army Distinguished Service Medal for his leadership of the 24th Division while in Korea.

After Korea, Church subsequently was appointed commandant of the United States Army Infantry School at Fort Benning, Georgia and served in that capacity until his retirement from the military in June 1952. He died on 3 November 1953, in Washington D. C. Survived by his wife, he was buried in Arlington National Cemetery, in Virginia.

Aftermath of the Korean War: The Geneva Conference (26 April -20 July 1954) was a conference which took place in Geneva, Switzerland, whose purpose was to attempt to find a way to settle outstanding issues on the Korean peninsula and to unify Vietnam and discuss the possibility of restoring peace in Indochina. The Soviet Union, the United States, France, the United Kingdom, and the People's Republic of China were participants throughout the whole conference while different countries concerned with the two questions were also represented during the discussion of their respective questions, which included the countries that sent troops through the United Nations to the Korean War and the various countries that ended the First Indochina War between France and the Viet Minh.

CHAPTER ELEVEN

THE VIETNAM WAR

Many American troops in Vietnam thought that the Vietnamese were Chinese, they were not. In 200 b.c. the first Chinese warlord journeyed into the Red River Delta, and the Chinese stayed for ten centuries.

The Vietnamese defeated them in Asia, and also beat the soldiers of the Tang dynasty and a century later defeated the troops of the Sung dynasty. By the seventeenth century Vietnam (meaning "Land of the South") extended its frontiers until the people were able to look over the Gulf of Siam.

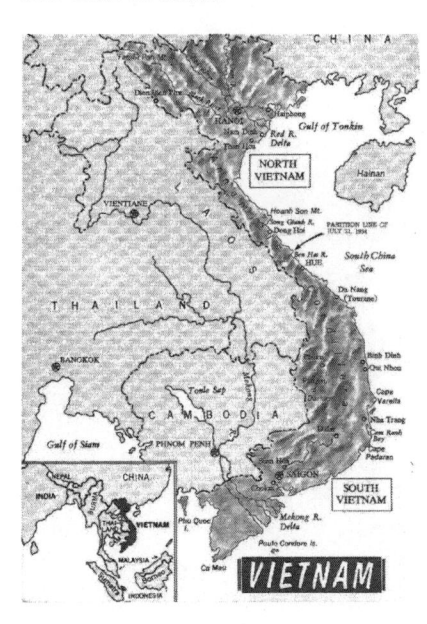

Also to the Vietnamese's disadvantage was the French who originally came to Indochina as missionaries in the 17th century, had made a fortune on the Vietnam rice, rubber and opium. They had driven the contented countryman to sell small holdings and to work in French factories and French plantations. The French did nothing to prepare the Vietnamese for independence. Having affirmed the ideals of an independent and civil unity, the Vietnamese faced the problem of translating into an effective government. This problem, however, could have been caused because of the rapid succession of rulers that passed through Vietnamese history unable to accomplish what was needed.

The French by the 1880's had completed their conquest and divided "Tonkin" into five colonial territories, Cambodia and Laos, Tonkin, Annam, and Cochin China, the last three comprising Vietnam. Making the capitol of Tonkin, Hanoi, the Central Annam and most populated part of Vietnam was governed from Hue. Cochin China, the Southern part of Vietnam, and the most French-influenced, had Saigon as its capitol.

In 1954 the Geneva Conference drew a demarcation line at the seventeenth parallel between Communist North Vietnam and Nationalist South Vietnam; not at the historic frontier but over sixty miles to the south at the obscure Ben Hai River. The line for the boundary left some 61,000 square miles to the north and 66,000 square miles to the south. The division once again called for two leaders, for North Vietnam Ho Chi Minh and Ngo Dinh Diem for the South of Vietnam.

Geography south of the Hoanh Son, the chains of mountains and plateaus of the Annamitic Cordillera close in toward the coastline. The plains are narrow here, and the old Vietnamese imperial capital of Hue lies on one of them; immured behind lagoons and dunes which discourage contact with the outside world.

South by train crossing "Cloud Pass"

A breathtaking Pass of Clouds between Hue and Da Nang, where the mountains end in the sea and fishermen spread their nets in the blue-green water far below, the plains broaden to form the most important rice field of central Vietnam. It is the most impressive railway journey in Vietnam.

The plains narrow again farther south, and the mountains join the sea once more at Cape Varella. The small plains which edge the lower central Vietnamese coast are separated by a series of mountain promontories, of which the most southerly is Cape Padaran. Turning eastward toward the sea is Central Vietnam, by the steep slopes of the Annamitic Cordillera mountain range which lies parallel to the coast land bars the way to the west. Only the narrow coastal corridors which begins south of Nha Trang links the people of central Vietnam with their countrymen who live beyond the Cordillera in the southern part of the country (the Nam Bo or Cochin China). This part of Vietnam shares the great rice and rubber bearing delta of the Mekong River with Cambodia.

Central, South and North Vietnam were known as Tonkin Annam and Cochin China for less than a century. It is therefore historically inaccurate to use these terms except during that relatively short time, from about 1884 to 1954, when Vietnam was a part of the French empire. But with the country now divided into the states of North and South Vietnam, the foreigner, to avoid confusion, is forced to make use of this convenient terminology.

The uneasy religious peace which prevailed during the nine years of the Diem regime degenerated into strained relations between government and the Buddhists during the last few months of the Diem regime. This regime ended in 1963 when Diem was assassinated. Since that time South Vietnam has experienced bloody clashes between the two organized religious communities; the Buddhists and the Catholics. This bitter hostility, however damaging, may prove to the immediate future of South Vietnam, and it may be expected to decline only with the reduction of the basic political tensions on which it feeds.

President John F. Kennedy and Vietnam

November 1960, the American people elected a new president. John F. Kennedy was the youngest person ever in the U.S. to be voted in to serve the American people; he became president at forty-three years of age. Kennedy was a Democrat and he would be replacing President Dwight D. Eisenhower known as "Ike", who would be finalizing his two term presidency of the Republican Party.

On 6 December, 1960, President Eisenhower met with his successor at the White House to discuss topics of importance that the going-out president felt necessary. After an hour and a half together, they were joined by Eisenhower's top cabinet officers for further discussions.

As preparation was being arranged for the new president's inauguration, the news traveled around the world, and wondering what the election of this young Democrat would mean for his country was Ho Chi Minh on the other side of the world. Ho was unsuccessful in engaging Washington's sympathies from Woodrow Wilson to Harry S. Truman. Now determined, had just delivered a speech in Hanoi that amounted to a declaration of war against the United States.

Eisenhower was preparing to leave office and dismissed Ho's threat as a last cry of an old radical. It was sad that Ho now seventy years was still fighting, and hoping for a united and independent Vietnam. Not long before his birth in 1890, the French had succeeded in a thirty-year campaign to claim all of Indochina as their colony. The French did not care about Laos or Cambodia, which had little value and that made up the Indochinese peninsula. Vietnam with its fine seaports and population became the center of French rule.

After the French quit Indochina in 1954, the United States assumed financial and military support for the South Vietnamese state. Clark Clifford was chief advisor in the transition period. The last meeting that Clifford arranged between the in-coming and the out-going presidents was held on 19 January 1961; Clifford was present taking notes.

Eisenhower started the meeting with the first item on his list; it was South-east Asia. With distinctive importance, he told Kennedy that he placed it first on the list because it offered the greatest danger to peace in the world. He ended his briefing on South-east Asia by saying that he felt the matter was so important that first we should call our member nation of SEATO (South East Asia Treaty Organization). He said at the very end and this is almost a quote – "If we cannot get our Allies to help us, then we must do it unilaterally."

Later Clifford became Secretary of Defense, and recalled Eisenhower elaborating on his domino theory: Meaning if South Vietnam fell, the next domino Laos, Cambodia, Burma, and on down into the sub-continent would go, the Philippines would go and possibly even Australia and New Zealand. The theory had a great impact on the new president.

In May, President Kennedy declared at a press conference that if necessary he would consider the use of US forces "to help South Vietnam resist Communist pressures. Vice-President Lyndon Johnson would leave for talks with Diem, in S. Vietnam. Following on 16 May, a fourteen-nation conference on Laos convened in Geneva, Switzerland and following it Kennedy and Soviet Premier Khrushchev personally met in Vienna to affirm Laos neutrality. Within five months the situation which Eisenhower had cited as reason for the US to go to war had been resolved.

Kennedy then called on President de Gaulle in Paris. De Gaulle told him: "The ideology that you invoke will not change anything, saying that you Americans wanted, yesterday, to take our place in Indo-China, you want to assume a succession to rekindle a war that we ended. I predict to you that you will, step by step, be sucked into a bottomless military and political cesspool.

President Diem sent President Kennedy a private-urgent letter, requesting a bilateral security treaty after a guerrilla force had ransacked a provincial capital only sixty miles away without resistance.

Torn by totally conflicting advice by both the military and political situation, Kennedy turned to General Maxwell Taylor, his personal military advisor. Showing Taylor the letter from President Diem, he asked him how he should answer it.

After consulting with Diem in South Vietnam, General Taylor reported back to the president. Taylor's recommendations, delivered personally to Kennedy in November 1961, included a combat commitment.

Kennedy's political advisor, Arthur Schlesinger Jr., says a specific proposal was for a force of 9 or 10,000 combat troops disguised as a flood control mission. Kennedy told Schlesinger he was very much opposed to this.

U. S. initiation into the Vietnam War...Within a few weeks Kennedy dispatched the first American helicopter units, called "Eagle Flights". The 300 American pilots were ordered to lead the Vietnamese into battle but not to engage in combat unless in self-defense.

The U. S. involvement escalated under the Kennedy administration through the MAAG (Military Assistance Advisory Group) program from just less than 1,000 to 16,000 in 1963. Also in 1963 the North Vietnamese had sent 40,000 soldiers to fight in South Vietnam. North Vietnam was heavily backed by the USSR and the People's Republic of China.

In August of 1963 tension reached a climax when government troops raided Buddhist headquarters at Xa Loi Pagoda in Saigon, (opposite photo showing Xa Loi Pagoda, which is a Buddhist landmark that consist of seven tiers and is the colorful center point of a well contained garden. The temple complex was built in

1956 and previously functioned as the headquarters of Buddhism in Southern Vietnam), and other pagodas which were also centers of agitation. The events intensified differences between Diem and the United States government which by then had taken the important step of replacing Ambassador Frederick Nolting with Henry Cabot Lodge in an attempt to transform Washington's policy into one of direct intervention in Vietnamese politics.

American impatience with Diem increased when it was learned that his brother Nhu was in contact with North Vietnam and with the Viet Cong insurgents and was seeking an agreement by which Hanoi would let the Viet Cong rebellion subside in exchange for a restriction of the American military presence in South Vietnam.

During President John F. Kennedy's years as president, he tripled the amount of American economic and military aid to the South Vietnamese and increased the number of U. S. military advisors in Indochina. He refused to withdraw from the escalating conflict in Vietnam because, he said, "to withdraw from that effort would mean a collapse not only of South Vietnam, but Southeast Asia also. So, we are going to stay there."

Some historians allege that just weeks before Kennedy was assassinated in Dallas, he supported a military coup that overthrew and murdered South Vietnam President Ngo Diem.

President Johnson and the Vietnam War - After President Kennedy was assassinated, the U.S. Presidency was turned over to Vice President, Lyndon B. Johnson, under the authority of President Johnson, the United States first deployed troops to Vietnam in 1965, in response to two separate attacks on U.S. Navy ships between Vietnamese and American forces in the waters of the Gulf of Tonkin that became known as the Gulf of Tonkin (for USS Maddox) incident. Initial reports from the United States blamed North Vietnam for the incident, but controversy suggests it was the blame of others for what took place on 2-4 August 1964. Also in response to the incident Congress drafted a Resolution (Public Law 88-40, Statute 78), that was proposed and approved on 7 August, 1964, as a joint resolution by Congress, that was enacted on 10 August.

The resolution carries historical significance because it authorized President Johnson to use conventional military force in Southeast Asia without officially declaring war. Specifically, it authorized the use of whatever force necessary to assist any member of the Southeast Asia Collective Defense Treaty of 1954.

Later, Congress under President Richard Nixon would vote to repeal the Resolution, which critics claimed gave the president a "blank check" to deploy troops and engage in foreign conflicts without officially declaring war.

United States Navy Seabees in Vietnam - In 1965 the steadily increasing insurgency of the National Liberation Army (Viet Cong), necessitated the large scale commitment of U. S. troops. Although Seabee teams had been active in the Republic of Vietnam since 1963, it was not until 1965 that larger Seabee units were deployed to aid in the Vietnamese struggle. Not since the Second World War had the need for the Seabees been so great and not since Korea had Seabees worked under enemy fire. On 8 March, 1965, 3,500 U. S. Marines landed near Da Nang in South Vietnam, thereby escalating the Vietnam Conflict and marking the United States' first action of the subsequent Vietnam War.

The first full Seabee Battalion; Mobile Construction Battalion Ten (MCB-10), arrived in Vietnam on 7 May 1965 to build an expeditionary airfield for the Marines at Chu Lai. MCB-3 followed shortly thereafter and provided a detachment to assist in the construction of the airfield. In 1965, the Seabee portion of the Vietnam construction program was concentrated at three northern coastal ports at Da Nang, Chu Lai, and Phu Bai.

At Da Nang the Seabees built three badly needed cantonments. Temporary facilities which included strong back tents, mess halls, shops, sheds, bathroom facilities, and a water distribution system were the first to be completed. In addition a SAM missile site had to be constructed overlooking the port of Da Nang. The Da Nang River Bridge had to undergo extensive repairs as well. Despite Seabee-built machine gun positions and bunkers for perimeter defense, one enemy attack succeeded in destroying the newly built advance base hospital, killing two Seabees and wounding over ninety. In true Seabee tradition, the men rapidly rebuilt the entire hospital complex.

While they are primarily builders and instructors, Seabee Team Members were sometimes directly involved in battle. Perhaps the most famous such battle occurred in June 1965, at Dong Xoai, 55 miles northeast of Saigon. When Viet Cong troops overran a Special Forces Camp obtaining 400 South Vietnamese and Allied Asian troops, 11 men of U. S. Army Special Forces team and nine men of Seabee Team 1104, seven of the Seabees were wounded and two killed. One of the dead was Construction Mechanic 3rd Class Marvin G. Shields, USN, who was posthumously awarded the Medal of Honor for conspicuous gallantry in carrying a critically wounded man to safety and in destroying a Viet Cong machine gun emplacement at the cost of his life. Not only was Marvin Shields the first Seabee to win the nation's highest award, but he was also the first Navy man to be so decorated for action in Vietnam. C.M. 3rd. Class M. C. Shields, home town was in Auburndale Florida; today the Florida Navy Seabee Veterans of America have dedicated and named a Navy Seabee Cadets Group in his name, "The Marvin Shields Sea Cadets" of Lakeland, Florida.

My second husband Lieutenant Kenneth Douglas Gammon, pictured; was a Company Commander in Da Nang, Vietnam, during the above period. Ken served in the U. S. Navy Seabees for twenty-two years. His military history is featured in my second book "A Salute to our Veterans" Vignettes of the "Can DO" Navy Seabees 1942-2007.

President Johnson's plan for Vietnam hinged on keeping U. S. troops south of the demilitarized zone separating North and South Vietnam. In this way, the United States could lend aid to Southeast Asia Treaty Organization (SEATO) without getting too involved. By limiting their fight to South Vietnam, U. S. troops would not risk more lives with a ground assault on North Vietnam or interrupt the Viet Cong's supply path running through Cambodia and Laos.

The United States took over the military training in South Vietnam; the first cost was $214 million. This million dollar-a-day went almost un-noticed in Congress related William Fulbright in late 1964. Also, American Ambassador in Saigon, General J. Lawton Collins, who had served during WW I, WW II and the Korean War, in the late 1950's was advising Washington that an alternative to Diem's government should be urgently considered; citing Diem's unwillingness to delegate authority, and the influence of his family. Diem appointed his brother as Chief Advisor, sister-in-law as official hostess, her father an Ambassador to the U.S., her mother as observer at the United

Nations, his other brother as Archbishop of Hue, two other brothers as regional overlords, with various cousins and in-laws as filling in cabinet and other posts.

Other qualified political and managerial personnel participated in the southern administration in good faith during the nine years of the Diem regime. After the assassination of Diem, during the rule of General Khanh, these leaders were either excluded from government service or persecuted because of antagonisms unrelated to their patriotism or their competence.

The Americans had encouraged the coup against Diem without making any preparation for filling the political vacuum created by that coup. Due to the error of the United States the leadership gap was widened. The period of demagogy ushered in by General Khanh's coup d'état against the military junta which replaced Diem completed the disruption of what had remained of the southern administration.

Khanh's rule, which was openly and clumsily supported by Washington, proved the most unpopular and disruptive of all the different regimes which have appeared since the November 1963 coup.

In the central highlands is a large region; the most promising for future economic development for Southern Vietnam, that appears to have created an ethnic problem, due to its occupancy by minorities that took apostate possession during the unrest in the country, representing a major danger to the unity of South Vietnam. Among other issues, the governmental instability; for instance the lack of incentive among potential leaders to assume political and administrative responsibility in Saigon. Also the unresolved movement between different religious groups, the Catholics, Cao Dai, Hoa Hao, and the Buddhists to name a few.

What the Vietnamese have going for them against all odds are sufficient enough to keep alive the eventually to promote the development of a non-Communist, independent, and a prosperous state of South Vietnam. The positive factors include the agricultural riches of the south; a relaxed, life-loving, courageous, and highly intelligent population; the continuing rise in political influence of a dedicated, politically aware elite persons of young army officers, and, above all, the undaunted spirit of nationalism and thirst for independence which, despite all calamities and reverses, has enabled the Vietnamese to survive for two thousand years.

Sergeant Charles L. Skipper: In my previous books, I have written about many of the stories that were told to me by the Vietnam Veterans, of which I have interviewed that had fought with the South Vietnamese during the Vietnam War. One veteran had given me a very detailed description of his journey while fighting that war. I have chosen his story because I feel that it describes/covers most of what the United States soldiers went through while they were overseas in that same country fighting the North Vietnamese.

It wasn't long after Charles had graduated from high school that the Vietnam War at its peak and the United States was drafting all the eligible men to train and go into combat. In his own words Charles tells about his military experience.

The war began for me on 26 May 1967; I was drafted into the Army and sent to Fort Benning, Georgia. There on Sandhill, I took basic training and was immediately sent through AIT, (Advanced Infantry Training) for Jungle Warfare. So from day one I knew where my destination was to be. Mid-October 1967, after a three week leave, in the early morning hours, I stepped from a plane at Cam Rhan Bay, South Vietnam into a wall of intense heat with a bad smell. After a week of getting used to the heat, bad smell and bad food, I was flown north from Cam Rhan Bay to An Khe. There I was assigned to D Company, 5th Battalion, 7th Cavalry, and First Cavalry Division. An Khe was a huge place, for it was the main base camp for the First Cavalry Division.

The western perimeter of the camp encompassed what was called Hong Kong Mountain. On the eastern side facing the camp all of the trees had been removed and a giant First Cav. Logo had been painted there. This was my first close encounter with the infamous Cav. Path, and it has been a part of me ever since.

For about three days we, the group I was with stayed around our battalion supply area where we turned in most everything that we brought with us and in turn we were issued our field gear and a weapon. I wasn't too sure about mine, an M-16. When you held it up and shook it the barrel would wobble to the left and right. To be honest I wasn't sure it would ever fire. During the day we helped around the supply area and got to check out the base. Some of these people didn't even know there was a war going on. There was a PX the size of any Wal-Mart where you could buy anything from a new car to you name it. Everywhere there were bars and nightclubs. What couldn't be found on the base could usually be found in the town of An Khe a short distance away.

One night we had to pull guard duty. We were placed out on the outer base premier at a guard tower. Just behind it was an old metal storage bin where we were to sleep. This was a trip; you had four brand new green grunts at a guard post for their first time. I don't think anyone went to sleep that night. So much for the good life.

Soon we were flying north and eventually landed in the Que San Valley, at a firebase named LZ Baldy. Que San Valley or as we called it Happy Valley lay a few miles South of Da Nang and ran East to West towards the border with Laos. The Valley was our brigade's area of operation; Baldy was the main support base for the area. Anything we needed or used usually came through there and out to the field. The other function of a firebase is the artillery support.

The Cav. always tried to operate under an umbrella of artillery. A huge advantage the Cav. had on other units that were air mobile, which meant with the helicopter support, at any time troops could be airlifted anywhere to engage the enemy or support other units. This also meant we could cover larger areas too. So to keep the artillery coverage each battalion would set up its own firebase. These were much smaller and could be moved fairly easily. All of the bases were called LZs (Landing Zones) and had a name. To us though, any place you could land a helicopter was a LZ.

A couple days spent on Baldy we stocked up on a few more essentials we needed, such as extra ammo, grenades, trip flares, some c-ration meals and a few other things that would come in handy in the days ahead. Next I climbed aboard a huey, a helicopter, for the first of many rides I would take. The huey was the Cav's lifeline. We depended on it for almost every aspect of our lives. It was our lifesaver if you happened to get hurt, it was our ride over rough terrain or for long distances, and it brought out supplies, food and water, for the most part it brought out two hot meals a day.

But this of course always hinged on the weather or our current situation. A very important thing to us was the fact that it was our link to the rear and the rest of the world. If you came or went in the Cav. you pretty much went on huey. Mail from home, what else I can say.

Most of us were young kids and away from home for the first time and news from family, friends and what was going on in the world was a great boost. This for me always seemed to keep me focused on the task at hand, so I would be able to go back the way I came, in one piece. I guess you could say life was good in the field. A short time into the trip, the chopper sat down beside a rice patty and I stepped off to my new home in the field, or as it was usually called, the boonies.

I had officially become a member of D Co. 5/7th Cavalry, and soon I became aware that I had stepped into a bit of history. This was the same 7th Cavalry that fought with General Custer at the Little Bighorn. This was in fact my new family. The platoon I was put in were all seasoned veterans who had been through some tough scraps and they knew their stuff and I quickly learned a lot from them. The major portion of my tour was spent here in the field and with the company. Everyone worked together and we shared all that we had.

After all we were pretty much self-contained; all we possessed was carried on our backs, so we didn't have many luxuries. Where we stopped at night we slept there. Unless we flew, we walked. I think the biggest luxury for me was having an air mattress that didn't leak or it was not raining.

During my tour I participated in four large campaigns of operations. Perishing, Jeb Stuart, Pegasus and Delaware. Operation Perishing was already in full swing when I joined the company. It was almost a year campaign; which was a series of search, and destroy missions. For this purpose we would move into an area and set up a base of operation. From there we would patrol the area in the villages, hamlets, roads, trails, rivers, or anywhere we thought we could find the enemy, make contact, and destroy them.

At times we would go into an area that had been declared a free fire zone. This meant that all of the friendlies had been told to leave so anyone left were considered the enemy and they were detained and sent somewhere in the rear. Also, we would go through the areas and destroy anything we thought would be helpful to the enemy. This would usually be food crops, rice, chickens, pigs, water buffalo, boats, bridges, or any weapons found. Usually in this area we were dealing mostly with the Viet Cong, (VC). They normally operated in small groups where they could hit and run easier. Given this fact we also worked in company and platoon sized units. Sometimes we would go on high ambushes called slashes. The VC liked to work at night so this was a way to disrupt their activities. From October until January this was how we worked dealing with small units of VC. The end of the year and into January we began to encounter soldiers in new khaki uniforms and more of them. These were NVA (North Vietnamese Army) soldiers.

This marked the beginning of a new era in the war. Large numbers of NVA troops had infiltrated south and on the first of February 1968, they launched a huge attack on the entire country. Every major city, town, and base was hit. With this, Operation Perishing was ended. The whole First Cavalry was ordered to pack up and move to the northern part of 1 Corps. This was the main operations area for the Marines, and we were to assist clearing out the enemy. This unit action was called Operation Jed Stuart, the TET Offensive.

A few miles South of Quang Tri City we took over a Marine base called Camp Evans and established the divisional base camp. From there we began our journey. Our battalion and another the second of the Twelfth Cav. 2/12 was sent south down Highway One to aid in the relief of Hue. This was the second largest city in South Vietnam. Overnight it seemed as though things had changed where we were working as a squad, platoon or company, now we were working as a battalion against NVA regiment and division sized forces. A couple of miles north of Hue we took our first test. A hamlet called Thon Que Chu was our objective. The NVA had established their regional headquarters in an Old French Bunker there and they had no intentions of leaving.

On 3 February 1968, the 2/12 had moved on the hamlet and soon became pinned down by intense small arms and mortar fire. Only after dark were they able to pull back to regroup. Twelve troopers who had been killed had to be left behind. It would be three weeks before they could be recovered. Now it was our turn, after scrapping our way down Highway One, we arrived at Thon Que Chu. We had heard about the 2/12 and we weren't too eager to take their place. Now the terrain was a major factor in this area. It was open rice patties with the hamlets and villages sitting on islands of high ground. These were usually two hundred to five hundred meters apart, so the only way to get from one to the other was across open ground. The NVA were well dug in with double trench lines and bunkers and it was to be no easy task to root them out. Our plan was to attack from another direction.

The first assault on 12 February 1968, we met the same fate as the 2/12. When we hit the wood line, we were hit hard and like 2/12, we had to pull back leaving our dead in the rice paddies. About dark we again tried to move in with the same results. So we pulled back to the hamlet behind us to wait. The three companies in the assault were hit hard with nine killed and 36 wounded. The fact that the dead were left and we couldn't retrieve them didn't sit well in the 5/7. We realized we were in a tough situation against a tough enemy and so came the name TT Woods, which is short for tough titty woods. We had a score to settle and on 21 Feb., we did.

At daybreak, A B Company lost its commanding officer (CO) and they pulled back, leaving us. A small tank called a duster that was sent to support us spotted the mortars and took them out. This took some pressure off of us and we worked our way forward and about noon two of our troopers were able to blow up the machine gun bunker that had everyone pinned down. This was the open door. C Company had moved to our right flank and B Company had rejoined us with the rest of the two companies close behind. We turned left down trenches clearing them and the bunkers out. By day's end the battle of TT Woods that had lasted for three weeks was over. We recovered our dead along with the 2/12 troopers. The bunker we were looking for we never saw. Another unit captured it.

The next day we were again moving south on Highway One into Hue. There was a small skirmish at the edge of the city. This was dealt with and then we slept in Hue. Daylight came and we again found ourselves in a different part of the jungle. This was a real city with real buildings. We would now experience the same thing the Marines coming up from the south would, house to house and street fighting.

What we learned yesterday didn't apply here. As all good troopers do, we adapted and worked our way south through small skirmishes until we met up with the Marines at the Perfume River. Unknowing to me, which I would find out years later, a friend of mine that I grew up with in a small Florida town, had joined the Marines and went to Nam at the same time as me, was standing on the other side of the river and we were looking at each other and neither knew it. The leaders up North had realized that the VC tactics weren't going to work so with the TET Offensive they had decided to go toe to toe with the Americans. This proved to be fatal, for not only did they lose all they had taken, but their casualties were quite severe.

Around the first week of March we found ourselves back at Camp Evans to regroup, rest and wait for what came next, which didn't take long. Even before TET the eyes of the world had been focused on a Marine base in the North West corner of the country called Khe Shan. The base was under siege by at least four enemy divisions. To most of the world this was to be our Dien Bien Phu.

The First Cav. had already been drawing up plans for a relief effort even before TET had hit. So came Operation Pegasus, the relief of Khe Shan. On 1 April the 7th Cav. led the way. From LZ Stud the 1/7 Cav. and the 5/7 Cav. air assaulted to each side of Hwy. 9, the road leading west to the base, and established two firebases, LZ Cates and LZ Mike. The 2/7 Cav. followed right behind the 1/7 on LZ Mike. The two bases brought Khe Shan and the areas around it under our support guns. The next day the 2/7 leaped farther west and set up LZ Thor. The second brigade came in on the third and fourth days with the 1/5 and 1/12 Cavs making LZ Wharton and the 2/5 Cav. set up LZ Tom. Days five and six brought in elements of the first brigade. The 1/12 and 1/8 Cavs set up LZ Snapper. The 1/12 Cav. left LZ Wharton and set up on Hill 471 west of Khe Shan. This leap frog tactic was a classic, for with each move we got close and eventually surrounded the base. This accomplished in just six days.

With the Cav. now in place we set out from each LZ to clear our respective areas. Our platoon for some reason was flown to an outpost on a mountain overlooking Khe Shan. I think they called it Hill 950. We replaced some Marines there. Looking down we had a bird's eye view of all the action going on below us. I don't know, but I am sure we surprised the NVA and even the Marines as to how quickly we came in and took control of the area. The contact we encountered was light to moderate, but the supplies and equipment we recovered were huge. By 10 April the siege was over and when we lifted off of the all-metal Khe Shan runway in C130 Cargo planes, Operation Pegasus was over. Of course a large Cav. patch was painted and left at the end of the runway.

Now it was back to Camp Evans for some down time. This time it seemed a little different. There were a lot of new faces among us. The two and a half months of fighting had taken its toll. Plus most of the guys who were here when I came in had already left or were going home. Now I was the old guy or veteran that all these new guys were counting on. After what I had been through and experienced for the last few months I felt like one. It didn't take the new guys long to get their feet wet. After a week and a half at Evans word came down to saddle up, we were on again. The brass decided we needed to hit the enemy one more time. This new operation was named Delaware.

We were to air assault into the A Shau Valley. The NVA had owned the valley and not since 1966 when a Special Forces Camp had been overrun were there any Americans present there. The enemy that was used to infiltrate men and supplies into the northern part of the country had built a large operations base. The terrain and weather would play a huge role as to how things went for us this time. The valley was skirted by high rugged mountains that often times reaches as high as 1,000 meters. The weather at its best was bad. Heavy clouds blanketed the entire area most of the time making visibility poor. These conditions made flying of any kind a challenging experience. Our aviation battalion, the 1/9, has to be highly commended for they never faltered. At least from us they received an A plus. To add to an already bad situation, for the first time we encountered anti - aircraft fire that had been dug into the mountain sides. The slow moving choppers laden with troops and supplies were almost sitting ducks. Even the support Cobras (gunships) were at high risk because the emplacements were well hidden and hard to find. On the first day alone, 23 choppers were hit with 10 of them being destroyed.

For us, the 5/7, again luck would smack us in the mouth. 19 April, our D Company air assaulted over the high mountains into the clouds, I had never done that before, and touched down in a small clearing on the side of a mountain where Hwy. 548 ran out of the valley floor up around the mountain and over into Laos. We were the first Americans in the A Shau in nearly two years. By the day's end our support guns were in place along with our other two companies A and C, and LZ Tiger was on line. The 1/7 had also come in on some slopes to our northeast and the next day other Cav. units were in place on the valley floor in the South.

To say the least, the A Shau was an uncomfortable place to be. The place had an eerie feeling to it. You felt as though everything you did was being watched not by someone, but by a lot of someone's. LZ Tiger sat two to three hundred meters up on the mountain over looking the valley floor. Our company took up positions along the road stretching two to three hundred meters above Tiger. We were about half way up to the top and the sides of the road were straight up and down. Literally we were sitting right on the road. In order to maintain our high ground advantage we really had no choice in the matter. Our company had now become the back door for this whole operation. If the enemy tried to send any reinforcements from Laos, they would be coming right through us to get to where ever they would be going. Another fact to ponder, below and into the valley, we had the big gun support from multiple Cav. units, and air strikes from fighter jets if needed. Being on the mountain and the way the road wound around, it would be difficult, if not impossible for most of that to be of use to us. To the west and on up around the road lay the great unknown. All we really knew was we were the end of the line. We had been dropped into the lion's den and we weren't real sure how hungry the lions were.

The weather was miserable; between the rain and clouds it was hard to tell which was which. Also, the bad weather hurt the supply system. The supply chopper at times was grounded and couldn't fly. A few days of being wet and eating c-rations put a hot meal on top of the luxury lists would be welcomed.

The platoons in our Comp, we encounter more and heavier contact. When contact down in the valley was made it seemed the enemy would break off and try to leave the area. So for someone seemingly trying to leave the area, these guys were putting up quite a fight to keep us from going around the mountain. Could it be there was something over there we weren't supposed to see?

The evening of 22 April, word came up to the platoon that division wanted me back in An Khe to attend a new leadership school. I was told that the new division policy was that all squad leaders were to be at least an E-5 rank (sergeant) or higher. Being an E-4, I was to attend the school and be promoted. This sounded good to me, for anytime spent out of the field was good time. Besides this was a chance to dry out and get some clean clothes maybe even a shower. I kind of hated leaving the guys (our platoon) given the situation we were in, but the rule out here is, if you can get out, go. The next day I would learn that I didn't have a choice. The next day 23 April on Tiger the Log Bird didn't show. The weather was bad and it would come when it could. So I waited. 23 April 1968, is a day that would be etched into history for D Co. 5/7 Calvary forever. Our company commander took part of the headquarters platoon and hooked up with the First platoon (my unit) and headed up the mountain. There was a finger slope jutting out that the road went around and each time it would be probed it drew heavy fire. This time instead of following the road he took his force up over the finger and down the backside. They found some communication cables on the ground so they knew they had found something big. We were getting close to something. As they moved down the slope near the road, they walked into the middle of a large bunker complex. Then things got bad. The two point guys were hit and went down, with the rest of the platoon in line behind them going for cover. Our platoon leader, his radioman, and another trooper were hit and killed. In the next few minutes a fierce firefight ensued. The gunfire and grenades that were thrown wounded the company commander, the company medic, and many of the other platoon members. In just a matter of minutes the platoon had been decimated.

The radios of Tiger were crackling and it was evident that these guys were in big time trouble. Fire support was out. As I had stated earlier it was only good into the valley. The cloud ceiling was so low up here that the Cobras would be too low and they could suffer the same fate. The Company executive officer (XO) got up a volunteer team, which I tried to join, but was told by the Company First Sergeant that he wasn't going against the division commander's order. He ascended the road at dark and brought everyone down except three of those that were killed. Repeated tries to retrieve them failed, even a scout helicopter went down with all lost in this effort.

The next day the weather was better and the log bird came along with some medevac choppers and I went out with the wounded. For their efforts the company executive officer won the Medal of Honor and some of the other rescuers won various other medals. The results of the fight above all others we were hit the hardest. In an instant we lost almost an entire platoon and probably if not for the rescue effort, all would have been lost.

What cuts the deepest is the fact that three troopers, six counting the chopper crew, never came home. He is still to this day a thorn in the flesh for us who were there. About a week later the Calvary pulled out of the valley and Delaware was over. I rejoined the company a week later around Camp Evans. Everyone was dry and resting. Again I joined new faces. This was now mid-May and it seemed that all was calm, at least for now. On 19 May, my squad walked into a minefield and myself and five others were wounded. Two were killed. Two weeks later I was on a medevac plane for the States. My fighting days and the war, as I knew it, were over. My tour lasted just a little over eight months. It sure seemed a lot longer especially the last four, it was as though we were in a four-month long running battle, and I guess we were.

I came in country a scared twenty-one year old kid and left a tired old man. I went back to Fort Benning, Georgia, where it all began. There I did my time on Kelly Hill with B Company, 5th Battalion, 31st. Infantry, and 197th Infantry Brigade. On 25 May 1969, I headed my new SS 396 Chevelle south towards Florida and my home. My army days were over.

Today as I look back on the war and all I experienced there I would not trade it for anything. I wouldn't want to do it again, but I didn't want to do it then either.

In February of 2004, I came in from work and I received a phone call that turned out to be quite a pleasant surprise to me. On the line was Mike Sprayberry. He was my Company XO and later my Company Commander in Vietnam. Mike is the one I had mentioned earlier that won the Medal of Honor in the A Shau Valley. Through Mike I found out that our 5/7 Calvary had its own Association, which I am now a member of.

You can read more about Charles Skipper and his Company Commander Mike Sprayberry, and his feelings about the Vietnam War, his feelings on how the troops were treated when they arrived home from fighting in the war, and how since then he feels about it all including his feeling about the Vietnam Wall. He had also written a verse in memory of, and dedicating it to all his Vietnam comrades. All can be found in my book titled; "A Salute to Our Veterans" Vignettes of Those Who Made the Difference 1939-2000, published in 2005). C.O. Mike Sprayberry also wrote the Forward in that book.

On 15 April 1967, Martin Luther King, Jr., (1929-1968) led thousands of demonstrators to the United Nations building in New York where the civil rights leader delivered a speech attacking the United States foreign policy in Vietnam; over 100,000 people attended the rally. King was a young Baptist Church pastor from Montgomery, Alabama who rose to prominence during the Civil Rights Movement; he remains to this day a symbol of the non-violent struggle against segregation.

Despite promises to bring a swift end to American involvement in Indochina, Johnson steadily increased the number of United States troops deployed to Vietnam, hoping to ensure a U. S. victory before withdrawing forces. No American president had yet "lost" a war, and Johnson hoped he wouldn't be the first.

By the end of his second term as president, his approval rates had plummeted and his hopes for bringing an end to the war in Vietnam had dissolved. On 31 March 1968, at the height of the Vietnam War, Johnson announced to the American people that he wouldn't seek reelection.

Another Vietnam Veteran that I had interviewed that told me about his experience while serving in the United States Navy Seabees is featured below.

Richard E. John – U.S. Navy Seabees was born in a small town in Osceola, Nebraska, on 13 January 1941 and grew up with his six siblings in Arcadia, Nebraska. His brother Robert was in the U. S. Navy and brother Wayne served time in the U. S. Air Force. He said that he had many cherished memories growing up and attending school in a one-room schoolhouse from first to the eighth grade.

Rick (the name everyone calls him) grew up on a farm that his father Albert Wilson John and mother, Lasca Wanna John managed. Rick also had a great-grandfather that served in the Civil War, his name was William Sarow, from his mother's side of the family, and he served with a regiment at Fort Kearney, Nebraska.

In 1959, after graduation from High School, Rick-John joined up with the United States Navy, he received his physical and written exam and then accomplished his Basic Training. He was given a choice in Boot Camp to go to the Fleet as a mechanic or be a mechanic in the U. S. Navy Seabees. He chose the Seabees.

Rick-John was sent to El Centro, California, Boot Camp where he was in a Transportation Unit. He had been told by everyone that he would have been better off as a driver, not mechanic. He took their advice and chose to be a driver for the rest of his career in the Navy Seabees.

It's amazing how many of the Navy Seabees that I interviewed had told me they don't know how to swim. When I interviewed Rick-John, he said that he didn't know how when he joined the Seabees and he had to learn, so he took swimming lessons while in Boot Camp.

I spoke to my husband about it, he had served twenty-two years plus in the Navy and was a Company Commander in Vietnam and never learned to swim, hummmm, I wonder if it's even required, you would think being they are on the water most of their enlistment. Just something to ponder!!

While serving in the Seabees, Rick-John was stationed in San Diego, CA, El Centro, CA, Coronado, CA, Davisville, RI, Great Lakes, ILL, Port Hueneme, CA, Guam and Vietnam. While serving he learned and used weapons' such as the M-1, 45-BAR-Mortar, his military occupation title was that of a Heavy Equipment Operator and he served with MCB#11 (Mobil Construction Battalion), 1960-62 and MCB#6 during the following dates, 1966-67.

Rick-John told me that while serving during the Vietnam War he remembered that a team of ten men and himself went from Da Nang to Chu Lai to repair the damage on the runway the North Vietnamese bombed. They were working one night and kept hearing a strange noise. Finally, he told the crew to take cover under the trucks. Ten minutes later it stopped and they were told that the Cong had sent mortars into the nearby Marine Camp.

After his honorable discharge Rick-John returned to Nebraska and worked on a road building crew, running a 31 yd scraper. In 1989 Rick-John moved his family from Massachusetts to Florida which is still his home state today. He is the father of two daughters, Linda John Buenavista, and Lanice John Jones.

He is a member of the VFW, Veterans of Foreign Wars, the NSVA, Navy Seabee Veterans of America, and the First Baptist Church of New Port Richey, Florida, where he and his wife Patty live and participate in Wing Man, a group that meets to learn how to be a better man in all areas of God and in his service.

Lieutenant William Calley, Jr. It's sad that all the Vietnam troops were blamed for what a very few United States leaders were guilty of during the Vietnam War. Namely one incident when the former lieutenant of the United States Army did during the Vietnam War. In 1971, was found guilty of murder for ordering the killings of hundreds of South Vietnamese civilians in the My Lai Massacre.

In March 1968, Lieutenant William Calley led his platoon into the hamlet of My Lai in South Vietnam. Suspecting the presence of Viet Cong fighters, Calley ordered his men to eliminate all inhabitants.

Hundreds of civilians, mostly women, children, and elderly men were killed, some of the women raped, and others mutilated.

Three years later, a military court sentenced Calley to life in prison for twenty-two murders. He appealed the conviction and was able to receive a reduced sentence. He was released from prison in 1974.

Richard M. Nixon – 37th President of the United States, Nixon followed President Johnson and took over the Vietnam War and continued to use the strategy of slowly withdrawing United States troops, so that the South Vietnamese troops could take over the fighting by themselves.

However, on 22 February 1969, one month after President Nixon's inauguration, a hundred towns and cities in the South came under prolonged assault in an echo of TET, a year earlier. During this time 1,140 Americans died. In retaliation, Nixon approved B-52 strikes against North Vietnamese sanctuaries inside Cambodia, and like former President Johnson's B-52 bombing in Laos and North Vietnam. The assaults were code named Operation Menu, as in luncheons at the White House. The first target was a North Vietnamese base area designated "Breakfast", this was to be kept top secret. Washington then waited for Hanoi's reaction before directing bombers at Lunch, Snack, Dinner, Dessert and Supper. There was no response.

Consequently, while the bombing was taking place, negotiations were under way in Paris; after taking several weeks to arrange seating between Saigon and the National Liberation Front (NLF) delegations, so to avoid face-to-face recognition and discussion. At the meeting Henry Cabot Lodge re-emerged once more as chief negotiator…and while the B-52s secretly bombed the Menu, Lodge secretly took tea with his Hanoi counterpart eleven times. Talks resulting always the same with the United States to first withdraw military, and then the two Vietnams would negotiate a political settlement.

Nixon's National Security Advisor Henry Kissinger, now privately appealed to Moscow (then providing North Vietnam with one billion dollars a year in aid) only to be told that the Soviet Union could not deliver an independent Socialist republic. When asked to define what influence Moscow had in Hanoi, a Soviet diplomat said "there is absolutely none."

Nixon secretly bombed many enemy targets in Cambodia and North Vietnam while bringing home the American troops; his justification was to make it easier for South Vietnam to win. When his spreading the bombing to Cambodia and Laos became known in 1970, it caused larger protests than ever in America. Including at Kent State and even in Washington, DC, where more than 12,000 were arrested in May 1971 at the peak of the protests. Partly because of the amount of opposition, Nixon sped up troop withdrawal and ended the draft.

Nixon was an American politician. He served as the 37th President of the United States, serving from 1969 to 1974, when he became the only president to resign. Before that, Nixon was a Republican, U. S. Representative and Senator from California and the 36thVice President of the United States (from 1953 to 1961) under President Dwight Eisenhower).

His presidency is known for a start for diplomacy with China, a slow ending of the Vietnam War, domestic acts (such as OSHA and the Environmental Protection Agency) and an era of peace with Soviet Union (Communist Russia). He is also known for corruption and the Watergate scandal which resulted in the public losing trust in him and his resignation.

Chief Kent Pfremmer – U. S. Air Force

In 1969 and 1971 – 2 Chief Pfremmer spent tours in Vietnam, before Kent served in Vietnam during the later part of his military career, he was active State-side in the preceding years before going over to Vietnam.

Often we read about veterans that have served their country in battles overseas, but never enough about the veterans that serve State-wide during the wars, and without them the whole war effort couldn't function. To make my readers aware of it I am including a veteran that served state side and in-country during the Vietnam War.

Kent was born in Lanesboro, Minnesota on 16 October 1939; he was delivered by his Uncle Bob, who arrived before the local doctor, at his grandfather's home. He was the oldest of seven siblings. He was baptized in a Lutheran church and attended a one-room school house in Minnesota along with his sisters Shelia, Barbara, Susan, Jackie, Gayle and Lisa and his brother Philip.

Kent came from a military family; in 1908 his grandfather served in the U.S. Marine Corps. During that period the Marines from 1900 thru 1916 participated in foreign expeditions, mostly in the Caribbean and Central and South America, including Panama, Cuba, Haiti, Santa Domingo and Nicaragua. Kent's father was a soldier in the Army during World War Two. His Uncle Bob served with the 6th Marine Division on Tarawa during that same war.

Kent was seventeen when he joined the Minnesota Army National Guard in Rochester, MN, in 1956. Kent transferred to the United States Air Force in October 1957. He attended Heavy Jet Aircraft Maintenance School and was assigned to the 346th Bomb Squadron, at Westover, AFB, MA. In 1961 Kent transferred to the 4047 Strategic Wing (later 306th Bomb Wing) McCoy, AFB, FL. In November 1964 he transferred to the 450th Bomb Wing at Minot AFB, ND.

While advancing his training in September 1965; Kent cross-trained into B-52 aerial gunnery. Upon completion of CCTS at Castle AFB he returned to 720th Bomb Squadron at Minot. After completing several school and CFIC courses while in Minot. In July 1968 Kent transferred to the 320th Bomb Wing, Mather AFB, CA as Stan/eval instructor.

In 1969, 1971-72 Kent did tours in Vietnam. Duty at Mather included four ARC-Light and one Bullet Shot tour in Southeast Asia. Sgt. Pfremmer was reassigned to Kincheloe AFB, MI. He was again Stan/eval instructor and squadron gunner while at Kincheloe. While stationed at the base, Kent and his family met and shook hands with President Gerald Ford. In 1975 Kent's next assignment was to the 17th Bomb Wing, Beale AFB, CA, to fill in newly created wing upgrade manager position. Pending Bomb Wing closure Sgt. Pfremmer became first sergeant of the Headquarters Squadron.

August 1976, Kent was transferred to the 28th Bomb Wing, Ellsworth AFB, SD, as wing upgrades manager. When promoted to Chief Master Sergeant (CM Sgt.), he became squadron gunner for the 37th Bomb Squadron. He later became wing gunner when that position became available.

CM Sgt. Pfremmer was reassigned to 319th Bomb Wing, Grand Forks, AFB, ND in January 1979 as the wing gunner, in October 1982 Chief Pfremmer was selected as senior enlisted advisor, 329th Bomb Wing, Kent remained in that position until retirement from active duty, 1 October 1986.

Chief Pfremmer spent his 29 plus years in Strategic Air Command. The only weapon system he maintained or flew was the B-52. Chief Pfremmer has over 5,000 flying hours, including 947 combat hours, with a total of 147 combat missions in Southeast Asia.

Chief Kent told me that one of the most difficult tasks he experienced during his military career was training technical systems to new students and imparting "team work" on multi-personnel crew. Although, he said he did enjoy the close knit attitudes of the people overall. He said that they knew the mission and did it.

In October 1986, Chief Kent Pfremmer was honorably retired at Grand Forks Air Force Base. For his thirty years plus of military service in the United States Air Force, Kent received a total of sixteen medals and ribbon decorations, including the Meritorious Service Medal w/one Oak Leaf Cluster and the Air Medal with six Oak Leaf Clusters, Vietnam Cross of Gallantry with Palm, Good Conduct, etc. He has flown every mode of the B-52 except the A and E. He is also featured in the Air Force Magazine "The Men behind the Guns", the History of Enlisted Aerial Gunnery 1917-1991.

While Kent was serving his country, so was his wife Marjorie She worked as a Civil Servant and when Ken retired from the military his wife Marjorie was offered and accepted a position in Hawaii. Kent then took a position with the Salvation Army in Hawaii as an Rehabilitation Manager. The following year Mrs. Pfremmer took a position at Langley AFB, Virginia and Kent found employment at the Post Office in Virginia, where he worked the next ten years before retiring.

In 1998 Chief Kent Pfremmer and Marjorie Pfremmer moved to Florida. They are the parents of three sons, Robert, Michael and Donovan, twelve grandchildren and six great-grandchildren. Their oldest son Donovan served with the United States Army for twenty-two years, during which time he was stationed at the DMZ in Korea and also served during the Gulf War and was an Army Recruiter for five years. He is now Safety Officer for the oil support company in North Dakota, and he and his wife have adopted six children.

Chief Prfemmer's son Michael also served in the U. S. military for five years as a classified soldier in Germany.

A Retired Chief, but keeping busy with social activities that include volunteering at his church, the American Legion, VFW, Eagles in Lakeland, The Elks, Bowling and the National Active and Retired Federal Employees.(NARFE). He is also a classic car buff and owner.

CHAPTER TWELVE

AMERICANS COME HOME FROM VIETNAM

The war for the US GI ends - Eight years of combat and a military involvement of some twenty years, the war for the Americans ended on 29 March 1973. In Hanoi on that date the last American prisoners-of-war were released and in Saigon the last token handful of GIs boarded a flight for home, 9000 miles away.

Up to that moment 56,962 American soldiers took their final breaths, they had died, most of them in combat in Vietnam (this figure is the most consistent that I have been able to find). Officially, the only US military personnel who remained in Vietnam were fifty advisors, as permitted under the Geneva Accords, of which the United States had refused to sign two decades before.

Unlike the military today, during the Vietnam War in the United States, our leaders were committing our young men to fight another country's war; they were drafted into it. Since then the United States has done away with the draft and the Arm Forces of America today are all volunteers.

Since the dedication of the "Wall" (National Vietnam Veterans Memorial) was dedicated, there has begun an essential healing process for many Vietnam Veterans to forgive and forget the unpleasantness that welcomed them during their homecoming from the war. Surely they know that not all Americans felt bitter or were bitter about that time in our history. And that the majority of Americans during the war and still today are proud of the men and women that fought during the Vietnam War, just as much as they are proud of the men and women that fought any of the other wars that the United States was involved in.

On the other hand we can understand your bitterness, hopefully your scars will heal in time, and you will forgive those that put them there. And know that in our hearts that we feel your suffering.

Vietnam Women's Memorial: On 11 November 1993 the Vietnam Women's Memorial was dedicated honoring women in military service during the Vietnam War. It was the first Memorial ever honoring female Military Veterans. It is located on the grounds of the Vietnam Veterans Memorial, the "Wall", in Washington, DC. Of the 265,000 women that served during the twelve years of the Vietnam War, none were drafted.

In September 1977, the North and South were officially united, becoming the Socialist republic of Vietnam, which was admitted to the United Nations—almost twenty-one years after the Geneva deadline for reunification. In those years Vietnam suffered as many as fifteen million dead and wounded; said Ha Van Lau, the veteran of Dien Bien Phu who became his country's Ambassador to the United Nations.

I am not going to pretend to know what caused the United States to ever get involved in that war in the first place. But, what I do know is that a country divided doesn't happen overnight, at first you don't see it, and suddenly it has happened. I shiver today when listening to the news and seeing how our own country has been getting divided among American democratic leaders, and I pray that it will get better and not end up in another American Civil War.

CHAPTER THIRTEEN

LEBANON – 1982-1983

In early June 1982, Israel invaded Lebanon and occupied it up to the capital city of Beirut where the Palestine Liberation Organization (PLO) had been headquartered. The Syrian forces that were stationed in Lebanon at the time fought the Israel invaders and lost several ground battles as well as over eighty Soviet-made Syrian warplanes that were shot down by the Israeli Air Force.

The Israeli troops continued the siege of Beirut and caused high volumes of civilian casualties. After an attempt in trying to negotiate a cease-fire with zero results, in August 1982, the American, French and Italian peace-keeping troops, otherwise known as the Multi-National Force (MNF) agreed to take up positions in Beirut between the PLO and the Israelis while the PLO evacuated Beirut for exile in Tunisia.

The PLO evacuation took place on 25 August 1982 with 800 U. S. Marines of the 32nd Marine Amphibious Unit (MAU), along with French paratroopers and 800 Italian military troops. The PLO evacuation took place with 8,500 Palestinian fighters shipping out to Tunisia, and 2,500 to other Arab countries.

After securing the country the U. S. Marines and the MNF troops left Lebanon. It wasn't long thereafter that they were called in again when two related events occurred and a new round of violence.

On 14 September the elected president of Lebanon, Christian politician Bashir Gemayel, was assassinated by a car bomb. And between the 16th and 18th of September, members of a Christian militia entered the Palestine and Lebanese camps of Shabra and Shatila in West Beirut and massacred hundreds of Palestinian and Lebanese Shiite men.

The U. S. Marines returned to Beirut on 29 September 1982, and joined the 2,200 French and Italian troops already in place in Beirut to begin training the Lebanese National Army (LNA). This military action turned into a conflict between the United States and Syria.

The middle of March 1983, eleven Italian troops and five U. S. Marines were wounded in a grenade attack that escalated on 18 April, when truck-bombs detonated by remote control exploded in front of the United States Embassy in Beirut, killing sixty-three embassy employees, including the CIA's Middle East director, and wounding one-hundred-twenty Hezballah.

Back and forth military actions continued during the summer, through September and into October, when on 23 October a suicide bomber drove a truck loaded with explosives into the lobby of the U. S. Marine barracks in Beirut, killing 241 Marines and wounding 81 others. The attack was carried out by Hezballah aided by Syrian intelligence and financed by Iran. This attack marked a turning point in the American presence in Lebanon.

American combat operations escalated in December 1983, when Marines at Beirut International Airport came under heavy fire from artillery in Syrian-held territory, killing eight and wounding two Marines. In retaliation American Naval Ships fired into the Syrian positions, and twenty-nine warplanes launched an attack on Syrian antiaircraft positions in the Shouf Mountains east of Beirut. Two United States warplanes were shot down by the Syrians.

CHAPTER FOURTEEN

GRENADA

In 1974, Grenada gained independence from the United Kingdom. In 1979, the Communist New Jewel Movement (CNJM) under Maurice Bishop seized power. Relinquishing the constitution and putting in custody several political prisoners.

In 1983, due to an internal power struggle over Bishop's foreign policy, a military group captured and executed Bishop and his partner Jacqueline Creft on 19 October. In addition, three cabinet ministers and two union leaders were also executed.

The United States being concerned over the 600 American medical students on the island at the time, the Reagan Administration authorized a military intervention following appeals by the Grenada Government-General P. Scoon.

Code-named Operation Urgent Fury the United States on 25 October 1983 led the Invasion into the Caribbean Island nation of Grenada; north of Venezuela. The assaulting forces, totaling approximately 7,600 troops were made up of the Army's Rapid Deployment Force, Army Delta Force, Navy Seals, Marines and Ancillary Forces together with Jamaican Forces and troops of the Regional Security System. A final assault took place by low airborne Rangers on Point Salines Airport at the south end of the island, and Marine helicopters amphibious landing on the north end of Pearls Airport took place.

The Rangers eventually secured True Blue campus and its students, where they found only 140 students and were told that more were at another campus in Grand Anse.

On the afternoon of 26 October, Rangers of the 2nd Battalion of the Ranger Regiment Mounted Marine CH-46 Sea Knight helicopters launched an air assault on the Grand Anse campus. The campus guards offered light resistance before fleeing, wounding one Ranger, and one of the helicopters crashed on the approach after its blade hit a palm tree. The Rangers evacuated the 233 American students by CH-53 Stallion helicopters, but the students informed them that there was a third campus with Americans at Prickly Bay. A squad of 11 Rangers was accidentally left behind; they departed on a rubber raft which was picked up by USS Caron at 23:00.

The 325th Infantry Regiment advanced toward Saint George, capturing Grand Anse and discovering 200 American students whom they had missed the first day. They continued to the town of Ruth Howard and the capital of Saint George, meeting only scattered resistance. An air-naval gunfire liaison term called in an A-7 air strike and accidently hit the command post of the 2nd Brigade, wounding 17 troops, one of whom died. Operation Urgent Fury ended and on 15 December 1983 and all forces had been withdrawn.

In the aftermath, Austin's military government was deposed and replaced by a government; appointed by Scoon.

Although the invasion was criticized by a few countries, including Prime Minister Margaret Thatcher. Thatcher was upset because she wasn't notified, but she did support the action. Also the Grenadian population approved of the Americans intervention, and appreciated the fact that there had been relatively few casualties, as well as the return to democratic election in 1984.

It amazes me that the United States is forever getting involved in other countries civil wars. Lebanon had been a civil war since 1975, between two different religious groups, that pitted the Lebanese Christians against Lebanese Muslims. And Lebanon is so far from our country, it's in ASIA, no less. In Lebanon 241 Marines were killed and another 81 wounded when the Marine barracks were bombed. Then we send students to Grenada. Grenada has problems with the government policies and a civil war starts, again American troops are sent in to restore diplomacy, and what happens, we lose American lives again, and Grenada is in the West Indies.

CHAPTER FIFTEEN

PANAMA – 1989-90

On 21 December 1989, President George H. W. Bush reported that he had ordered United States military forces to Panama to protect the lives of American citizens and bring General Noriega to justice. The operation was named, Operation Just Cause.

United States concern was due to the circumstance that it maintained military bases throughout the Canal Zone. The agreement between U. S. President Jimmy Carter and General Omar Torrijos back in September 1977 set the motion for the U. S. handing over the Panama Canal to Panamanian control by 2000. One condition of the transfer was that the canal would remain open for American shipping.

Relations between General Noriega and the United States began to deteriorate in the mid 1980's. In 1986, U. S. President Ronald Reagan opened negotiations with General Noriega, requesting that the Panamanian leader step down after he was publicly exposed in the New York Times by Seymour Hersh, and was later implicated in the Iran-Contra Scandal along with other drug related indictments.

In May 1989, during the Panamanian national elections, the election results showed that an alliance of parties opposed to the Noriega dictatorships candidate, that Guillermo Endara, defeated Carlos Duque, candidate of a pro-Noriega coalition by one to three. Guillermo was physically assaulted by Noriega supporters the next day in his motorcade. Noriega declared the election null and maintained power by force, making him unpopular among Panamanians.

The Panamanian general assembly met on 15 December and passed a resolution that a state of war existed between Panama and the United States. The United States reinforced its Canal Zone garrison, and increased the tempo of training and other activities intended to put pressure on Noriega.

The following day, 16 December, four military personnel were on their way to Panama City when their vehicle was ambushed by Panamanian Defense Forces (PDF). One of the officers, Lieutenant Paz, was fatally wounded, the driver of the vehicle was wounded in the foot, and all were arrested. The next day President Bush ordered the execution of the Panama invasion plan; the military set H-Hour as 0100 on 20 December.

The U. S. Invasion of Panama codenamed Operation Just Cause occurred between mid - December 1989 and late January 1990. During the invasion Dictator Manuel Noriega was deposed, president elect Guillermo Endara was sworn into office, and the Panama Defense Forces was dissolved.

CHAPTER SIXTEEN

THE GULF WAR

August 1990, Codenamed "Operation Desert Shield", also known under other names as the Persian Gulf War, Gulf War One, Kuwait War, First Iraq War, all before the term "Iraq War" became identified.

In 1980, the United States kept quiet after Iraq invaded Iran, marking the beginning of the Iran-Iraq War. The cause that troubled the U.S. not to interfere is that Iraq had been a colleague of the Soviet Union, a country that the U.S. had difficulties with. And also because of the support that Iraq gave to many Arab and Palestinian combatant units such as Abu Nidal. Although, the United States remained steadfast as far as joining the action, it did supply political support and some aircraft to Iraq.

The United States knew Iraqis were doing their best at fighting with Iran and so the US increased its support to insure that the Iraqis didn't surrender.

95,000 Iranian child soldiers were made causalities during the Iran-Iraq War, mostly between the ages of 16 and 17, with a few younger.

By the time that a cease-fire was signed in August 1988, Iraq was deep in debt to Saudi Arabia and Kuwait.

In 1989, it appeared that Saudi-Iraqi relations strong during the war would be maintained. A pact of non-interference and non-aggression was signed between the countries, followed by a Kuwaiti-Iraqi deal for Iraq to supply Kuwait with water for drinking and irrigation, although a request for Kuwait to lease Iraq Umm Qasr was rejected. (Umm Qasr, is a port city in Iraq that leads to the Persian Gulf. It is separated from the border of Kuwait by a small inlet). Prior to 1991, and the Persian Gulf War, a bridge across the waterway linked the port with Kuwait.

In mid-1990, Kuwaitis were threatened by Iraq for not keeping to their allotment and said that they would take military action.

The United States Naval fleet in the Persian Gulf was alerted when it was reported that 30,000 Iraqi troops had moved to the Iraq-Kuwait border.

On the 2nd day of August 1990 the Iraqi Army invaded and occupied Kuwait. The Iraqis had gone straight into the city of Kuwait, surrounded it, then cut off Kuwait City from the countries southern half. The Royal family escaped leaving the Iraqis in control.

The Kuwait armored battalion, 35th Armored Brigade, was deployed against the Iraqi attacks and was able to conduct a vigorous defense at the Battle of the Bridges near Al Jahra, west of Kuwait City. Also, Kuwaiti aircraft whirled to meet the invading force, along with combat attacks flown against Iraqi ground forces.

Iraqi commandos deployed by helicopters and boats attacked the city from the sea, while other divisions seized the airports and two airbases. The Iraqis attacked the Dasman Palace, the Royal Residence of Kuwait's Emir, Jaber Al-Ahmad Al-Jaber Al-Sabah, which was defended by the guards and supported with M-84 tanks.

Within twelve hours, resistance in Kuwait ended; most of the Kuwait troops were either conquered or escaped to Saudi Arabia. After Saddam Hussein's guerillas took over Kuwait, he created a regiment known as "Provisional Government of Free Kuwait" and assigned his cousin Ali Hussein as governor, on 8 August1990.

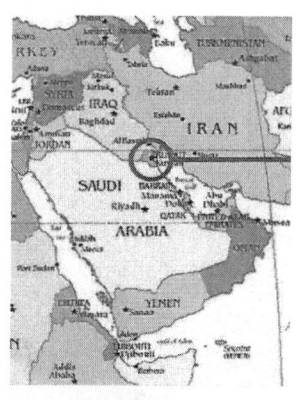

The next few days Kuwait and United States requested the United Nations Security Council (UNSC) pass a resolution demanding a withdraw of Iraq troops.

On 6 August 1990, Resolution 661 placed economic sanctions on Iraq, and Resolution 665 followed, authorizing a naval blockade to enforce the sanctions.

The United States had been uncertain as to whether it should get involved; until the UK Prime Minister Margaret Thatcher reminded President Bush what had lead to World War Two. That Saddam could take over the whole gulf and all oil rights if not stopped.

From the beginning of August through to November 1990, Saddam and the US went back and forth with proposals, with no results. Then on 29 November, Resolution 678 was passed, which gave Iraq until 15 January 1991, to withdraw from Kuwait and authorization to use whatever means necessary to evacuate Iraq out of the city of Kuwait after the deadline. Although Saddam wanted to negotiate with the UK and US, the countries stuck to their proposals and said that no negotiation until Iraq withdrew from Kuwait.

Soon Saddam began attacking the Saudis. During the Iraq War against Iran, Saudi Arabia backed Iraq. After the war Saddam refused to pay back loans due to the help he had given the Saudis by fighting Iran.

OPERATION DESERT STORM - Suspecting what Saddam was working up to; U. S. President Bush announced the United States would launch a "wholly defensive" mission to prevent Iraq from invading Saudi Arabia under Code name "Operation Desert Storm".

The expense of any military action is very, very costly, so to ensure the economic support of "Operation Desert Storm", James A. Baker, III, Secretary of State, USA, went on an eleven day tour, starting in September 1990, to visit eleven countries for financial and military troop support. The press called it "The Tin Cup Trip".

The first stop on the way was Saudi Arabia, who had already, one month earlier granted US the use of their facilities. Since the militaries important objective was to defend Saudi Arabia, Baker asked King Fahd for 15 million dollars, the King agreed, with the promise that he would ask Kuwait for the same amount. The next day Mr. Baker met with the Emir of Kuwait outside his hotel, he easily agreed to the amount.

Secretary Baker traveled on to Egypt, and spoke to the Egyptian President Mubarak, who was furious with Saddam's invasion of Kuwait, and agreed to support the action. After stops in Helsinki and Moscow, Baker carried on to Syria and visited with President Hafez Assad. Assad agreed to pledge up to 100,000 Syrian military troops.

Mr. Baker flew to Rome and visited with the Italians and was promised the use of some military equipment, then traveled to Germany to meet with American ally Chancellor Kohl. Kohl committed to a 2 million dollar contribution to the Coalition's war effort.

Although Japan and Germany could not contribute forces, they made contributions of $10 billion and $6.6 billion. The United States represented 73% of the Coalition and placed 956,600 troops in Iraq. And the day before ground forces began, the World Bank gave Iran the first loan of $250 million.

The Coalition of forces opposing Iraq's aggression was formed consisting of forces from thirty-three countries. The US Senate supported the military action with a vote of 52-47. United States Army General Norman Schwarzkopf, Jr. was appointed as Commander of the Coalition Forces in the Persian Gulf Area.

President George Bush deployed United States forces into Saudi Arabia, and urged other countries to send their own forces to the scene. A large amount of countries joined the coalition, forming the largest military alliance since World War II.

On 17 January, the Gulf War began with aerial bombing. For forty-two days and nights the coalition forces subjected Iraq to the most intensive air bombardments in military history. They flew over 100,000 attacks, dropping 88,500 tons of bombs. The air campaign was commanded by USAF Lieutenant General Chuck Horner.

The day after the deadline set in Resolution 678, the forces engaged in a large air campaign, Codenamed "Operation Desert Storm"

Five hours after the 1st attacks, Iraq fired eight missiles. Following the first Israeli Air Force jets were deployed to patrol the Northern air space with Iraq. Israel prepared to retaliate, however, President Bush pressured Israeli Prime Minister Shamir not to retaliate and to withdraw its jets. Israelis grew impatient as the Scud attacks continued and considered taking the Iraqis out. On 22 January 1991, a missile hit a small Israeli city, after two Coalition patriots failed to intercept it.

The Israelis grew more impatient. The Iraq force attacked the Saudi city of Khafji on 29 January 1991, which was lightly defended, the battle ended two days later when the Iraqis were driven back by Saudi Arabian National Guard, supported by Qatari forces and US Marines.

On 15 February 1991, Task Force 1-41, the first coalition force to breach the Saudi Arabian border was a US Army Heavy Battalion Task Force from the 2nd Armored Division (Forward). It was the spearhead of VII Corps, of the 1st Battalion, 41st Infantry Regiment, 3rd Battalion, 66th Armored Regiment and the 4th Battalion, 3rd Field Artillery Regiment engaging in direct and indirect fire fights with the enemy on 17 February.

On 25 February 1991, a Scud Missile hit a US Army Barracks of the 14th Quartermaster Detachment out of Greensburg, Pennsylvania, Stationed in Dhahran, Saudi Arabia killing 28 soldiers and wounding over 100.

It was decided to send British Armored force into Kuwait fifteen hours ahead of schedule, and to send US Forces after the Republican Guard. Proceeded by a heavy artillery and rocket barrage, after which 150'000 troops and 1,500 tanks began to advance towards the city. Despite the intense counterattack against US troops, the Americans repulsed the Iraqis and continued toward the city of Kuwait, and quickly liberating the city.

On the 27th day of February 1991, Saddam ordered a retreat from Kuwait and President Bush declared it liberated. After four days of fighting, the Iraqis were kicked out of Kuwait. As part of a scorched earth policy, the Iraqis set fire to nearly 70 oil wells and placed land mines around the wells to make extinguishing the fires more difficult.

Kuwait was liberated and the forces advanced into Iraqi territory. One hundred hours after the ground forces started, a ceasefire was declared. On the 28th day of February 1991, a Cease-fire term was negotiated. The first day of March 1991, Iraq officially accepted a Cease-fire. Also on the 28th of February 1991, President George Bush declared that Kuwait had been liberated.

For my Desert Shield and Desert Storm Warrior I am going to introduce you to a special lady that served during the Gulf War, in Desert Shield and Desert Storm. And that I had the opportunity and privilege to interview.

Kathryn A. Gates Skipper, Staff Sergeant

United States Marine Corps – Desert Shield & Desert Storm. Kat was born on the shores of Tripoli, 19 September 1957 and considers herself a true Marine. She was adopted by an Air Force Master Sergeant (later Colonel), of Chicago and his wife Nellye, who was born in Mississippi. The adoption took place while they were stationed at Wheelers Air Force Base, Tripoli, North Africa. Her new name was

Kathryn Ann Peters. (Wheelers AFB is now an air base turned over to the Libyan government.)

Tripoli is the capital of Libya, the State of Libya is a country in the Maghreb region in North Africa, pictured below.

When Kat was eight months old, they were transferred back to the US, at Camp Perrin Air Force Base, Sherman, Texas. The end of October 1961, her father passed away.

Kat and her mom moved to the base at NAS Millington (Memphis, Tennessee), where relatives lived. Her mom met Larry "Mac" who was stationed in the Navy and taught Naval Aviation at the base. Nellye, Kat's mom, and Mac were married and Kat had a new father.

While in Texas, Kat attended the Lucy Elementary School, and when her dad retired from the Navy in 1968, they moved to Pickwick Damn, Savannah, TN.

Every year the family would take a vacation in the Florida Keys, where they enjoyed going fishing. When Kat was in high school the family moved to the Florida Keys. After completing high school, Kat attended college back in Memphis at the University. She wasn't happy in college so she decided to join the US Marines in November 1975. She served in the administration field of the Marine Corps. It wasn't her first choice, but due to the situation that her first choice, the aviation field was frozen; her second was available at the time.

To her surprise, one week after she passed her physical and examination she was shipped out to Paris Island in South Carolina. It would be her first holidays away from home, Thanksgiving, Christmas, and New Years.

Kat said that she remembered while being at basic training that she was interviewed by actress Candice Bergen for a documentary on Women in the Marine Corps. And Kat also stated that Paris Island was a flea island; and if you happen to swat one while standing at attention, the DI's would make a big issue about it with a burial ceremony and so forth.

After graduation in January 1976, Kat's first duty station was at Camp Lejeune, Jacksonville, North Carolina, assigned to the Marine Corps Engineer School, Courthouse Bay.

During her tour she was one of the first women Marines to participate in combat exercises and stay overnight in the field. Before that, women were not allowed to participate in any type of combat/

training exercise. Fortunately, changes were taking place while Kat was serving in the Marines.

While stationed at Camp Lejeune, Miss Peters met and married her first husband (Greg), who was the base career planner. Two years later they separated. The winter of 1978 was cold she recalled, that is when she had to qualify on the rifle range, and made Expert.

She was stationed there four years, her entire enlistment. When her enlistment was up in November of 1979, Kat took a position that she was offered in New York City, in the Paymasters Department, as an assistant to the vice president. During that period she also went to modeling school and was able to work part-time modeling for Macy's and Bloomingdales. She was also active in the Marine Corps Reserve's "Toys for Tots" Campaign and was featured on the cover of the Marine Corps Dixie Digest in January/February 1980.

In the fall of 1980, she and her husband reconciled and she became pregnant with her only child and moved back to Camp Lejeune, North Carolina, where he was stationed. Kat joined the reserve unit in Cherry Point, NC and went back to college.

On 5 June 1981, her son was born-Gregory Lynn Gates, Jr. The following year, her husband was transferred to Iwakuni, Japan, but their son and Kat stayed in NC, so that she could finish college. Kat and her husband Greg separated again and after graduating college in 1983, she moved back to Florida with her son.

Back in Florida and living in Haines City, also, because she was a Marine reservist, she was assigned to the Marine Corps mobilization station in Jacksonville, FL. During which time she was employed part-time at Disney World and worked at the local bank. Kat also kept busy doing some modeling and acting part time, she did a few TV commercials, HBO movie, and the TV show Miami Vice.

She and Mr. Gates finally were divorced. The following year, she lost her Navy dad of natural causes. For the next several years, Kat did a lot of special projects for the Marine Corps, doing active duty here and there, from Twenty-Nine Palms, CA to Overland Park, Kansas.

In January 1991, Kathryn Ann Gates was activated for Desert Storm. Leaving her ten year old son with her mother, Kat went to war. She was assigned to JSPE Depot (Joint Services Personal Effects) at Fort Dix, New Jersey. The base had been closed for some time but was reopened for this war. She was assigned to a unit that was mostly Army, with an Army commanding officer, but there were a handful of Navy, Air Force and Marines in the unit. The unit was in charge of all the personal effects of the casualties. She stated that the job was much harder than working at the Mortuary Affairs Depot in Dover, Delaware, where the deceased bodies were. It was their job to return EVERYTHING of the deceased's belongings to the family.

There were young Kuwaiti soldiers that were going to college in the US, and they trained for war there. The first graduation of these soldiers was held at Fort Dix, NJ.

Kat said that she helped train the female Kuwaiti soldiers and was on CNN News together with them.

Kat volunteered to go in country to make sure all the personal effects of the casualties were accounted for, as the war was about to end. She stated it was really scary, with scud missiles flying in the air and anything could have happened. But, as a Marine, she said she had to tough it out! She was counting her blessings that it was a very short tour. Returning to the states Kat was sent to Camp Lejeune, NC, to help process discharges from the war. She hadn't been there for over ten years and noticed many changes at the base.

At the end of the summer, she was released from active duty and transferred to the reserve unit in Tampa, FL. The town of Lakeland, FL was giving a BIG hero's welcome home parade to the local National Guard unit returning from the war. And she said that she received a telephone call from an angel of mercy who found out about her returning home, and told her that they wanted to honor her in the parade. She said that she was overjoyed and in tears. After three more years in the reserves, Kat got out to take care of her mom who had a second bout with cancer. On 13 June 1995, Kat said that she lost her best-friend her mother.

Kat worked for a cable company for a while, and then started her own business, "KAT AND SON TRANSPORTATION".

When 9-1-1 hit, Kat's son Greg joined the Navy and Tampa Bay 28 News went to her home to interview her and her son, about a "mom and son" military team. Greg's tour of duty was spent on the USS Kitty Hawk in Yokusko, Japan.

In February 1999, Kat went out on a date with her future husband, Charles, whom she had met a year earlier. On the 26 day of March 2005, Charles Skipper and Kathryn Ann were married. Charles had served in the Army, with the 7th Cavalry, and was stationed in Vietnam during the war and is featured in this book.

Recently Kathryn "KAT" Gates - Skipper was selected to "Veterans Hall of Fame" in Lake Wales, Florida, with a half-page write-up in the Lakeland Ledger Newspaper.

Following her military career, she raised awareness of issues affecting the US veteran population. A volunteer for- concerned Veterans of America, she eventually became the group's Central Florida field service director and helped pave the way for passage of the VA Accountability Act of 2014.

Kat has been the Judge Advocate for the Local Marine Corps League, Heart of Florida Detachment since her release from active service. Her mission to help veterans started 18 years ago, while she was helping her husband with post-traumatic stress disorder, he had received two purple hearts.

During her career Kathryn A. Gates-Skipper was awarded the Army Achievement Medal, the Meritorious Unit Commendation, Marine Corps Good Conduct Medal, National Defense Service Medal, SW Asia Service Medal, Navy & Marine Corps Overseas Service Military Ribbon, The Kuwait Liberation Medal, (Saudi Arabia), Marine Corps League Distinguished Service Award, the State of Florida Governor's Veteran Award, the American Legion Veteran of the Year Award and other commendations, with Ribbons and Stars.

Kat is still pressing forward as an advocate for veterans. She advocated getting the VA Mission Act passed, an act that will give veteran's greater access to health care by going to a civilian doctor instead of waiting thirty days to go to a VA doctor. The Hall of Fame is located in Tallahassee, for a list of all inductees, visit florida-vets.org/our-veterans/florida-hall-of-fame. To learn more about Mrs. Skipper, her entire military experience and more is featured in my first book "A Salute to Our Veterans" Vignettes of Those Who Made the Difference 1939-2000.

Saddam Hussein: In 1991 when the Gulf War ended Hussein was suffering from defeat. His regime accepted the conditions for a cease fire, expressed in the United Nations Security Council, Resolution 686. Also he agreed liability for any loss or injury as a result of its invasion and occupation of Kuwait.

In April of the same year, the UN Security Council passed its Resolution 687, demanding that Iraq destroy, remove and render harmless its weapons of mass destruction and ballistic missiles with range of more than 150 kilometers. And it should be done so under international supervision.

Rather than comply with the Resolution 687, an estimated report suggests that in 1991-92, Hussein chose to destroy biological weapons and chemical weapons. But had frozen scud missiles that were capable of reaching 600 miles, more than allowed by the Security Council resolution.

While UN inspectors were in Iraq monitoring verification plans and Hussein complained, and so his conflict with the United Nations Security Council grew. United States and Britain remained hostile toward Hussein through 1992, and relations did not improve through April 1993, when it was alleged that the Hussein's regime had attempted to assassinate the former US President, George Bush, while visiting Kuwait as a private citizen. After which, President Clinton ordered ships to launch Tomahawk missiles against the headquarters where it was thought the Iraqis had plotted the assassination.

Bosnia – 1991-1992, the United States policy makers during the Bush administration did not view the US as having any interest in the Bosnia conflict that would involve the American military.

In mid 1993-1994, the Clinton administration policy changes included the United States were more involved in an attempt to consider more forceful measures to end the fighting and human fatalities occurring in the Bosnia battles. The results were negative.

Then in 1994-95, the United States seeking a negotiated end to the war used forcible diplomacy and the North Atlantic Treaty Organization (NATO) airpower against the Bosnia Serbs and their allies in Belgrade that ended in the Dayton Accords, a peace agreement by the presidents of Bosnia, Croatia, and Serbia at the end of 1995 ending the war in Bosnia.

In March 1995, Bosnian Serb President Radovan Karadzic orders that Srebrenica and Zepa, (Zepa is a small town on the Zepa river on the outskirts of Eastern Bosnia) be entirely cut off and aid convoys be stopped from reaching the towns.

On the 9th day of July, Karadzic issues a new order to conquer Srebrenica.

On 11 July, Bosnian Serb troops, under the command of General Ratko Mladic, capture the eastern enclave and United Nations; "safe area" of the Srebrenica, killing about 8,000 Muslim males in the following week. The U. N. war crimes tribunal in The Hague indicts Karadzic and Mladic for genocide in the siege of Sarajevo.

Following the NATO air strikes against Bosnian Serbs, in November, Bosnian Muslim President Alia Izetbegovic, Croatian President Franjo Tudjman and Serbian President Slobodan Milosevic agree to a United States brokered peace deal in Dayton, Ohio.

On the 14th of December the three leaders signed the Dayton Peace Accords in Paris, paving the way for the arrival of a 66,000-strong NATO peacekeeping Implementation Force in Bosnia. Therefore the international community establishes a permanent presence in the country through the office of an international peace overseer.

In July of 1996, West forces Karadzic to quit as Bosnia Serb President. In September, Nationalist parties win first post-war election, confirming Bosnia ethnic division.

In 1997, having lost power, Karadzic goes underground. And from 1996-97, the United States provided leadership of, and participated in the NATO ground force which implemented successfully the military provisions of the B-Dayton Accords.

On 25 September 1997, Turkish forces re-entered Iraqi Kurdistan and attacked the Patriotic Union of Kurdistan (PUK) and Headquarters of the Kurdistan Workers Party (PKK) positions in an attempt to force the PKK to leave Iraqi Kurdistan. However, according to Turkish sources, it was an attempt to bring a cease-fire between the factions. The operation resulted in heavy PKK and PUK casualties. Later a cease-fire was negotiated between the PUK and Kurdistan Democratic Party (KDP) and the United States (US) decision to support a cease-fire.

The 7th day of November 1997, United Nations envoys ended their diplomatic mission to Baghdad with no signs that Iraq would back down in its standoff with American arms inspectors. The three-man delegation representing the United Nations (UN) secretary-general hailed the positive atmosphere of the talks.

The tension between the United States and Iran was especially noteworthy in Iraq, where about 5,000 U. S. troops are deployed ostensibly to aid the Iraq fight against the Islamic State. On the 24 of November, the KDP declared a unilateral cease-fire. The PUK, although not declaring a cease-fire officially, said their group would respect the truce, despite alleging that the KDP had violated the truce by attacking PK positions on 25 November.

AFTERMATH - In September 1998, Barzani, leader of the Patriotic Union and Talabani, President of the Democratic Party, signed the United States mediated Washington Agreement establishing a formal peace treaty. In the agreement, the parties agreed to share revenue, share power, deny the use of northern Iraq to the PKK, and not allow Iraqi troops into the Kurdish regions.

The United States pledged to use military force to protect the Kurds from possible aggression by Saddam Hussein. At the same time, implementation of the United Nations Oil-for-Food Program brought revenue to northern Iraq, allowing for increased standards of living. Becoming a peaceful region, before the small terrorist group Ansar al-Islam (the group call themselves Sunni Muslim insurgents, they are in Iran and Syria) entered the Halabja region in December 2001.

CHAPTER SEVENTEEN

SEPTEMBER 11, 2001-9/11

<u>A day that will live in infamy</u> - The United States was attacked by terrorists at 8:45, Tuesday morning, on September 11, 2001, in Manhattan, New York. The World Trade Center was attacked. The media described it as "Terror at Home", "Act of War", "World Trade Center Destroyed", "Many Dead", and "Death of the World Trade Center".

The first plane, a Los Angeles American Airline Flight 11, Boeing 767 aircraft, departed Logan Airport at 7:57 a.m. en route to Los Angeles with a crew of 11 and 76 passengers, not including five hijackers, crashed into the upper half of the North Tower of the World Trade Center, New York City at 8:46 a.m.

Eighteen minutes later a second plane, United Airlines Flight 175, a Boeing #767 aircraft, departed Logan Airport at 8:14 a.m. en route to Los Angeles with a crew of nine and 51 passengers, not including five hijackers, slammed into the mid-section of the South Tower at 9:03 a.m., sending a massive fire ball ripping through to the other side of the building.

The third attack, American Airlines Flight 77, a Boeing 757 aircraft, departed Washington Dulles International Airport at 8:20 a.m. en route to Los Angeles with a crew of six and 53 passengers, not including five hijackers. The Kamikaze flew the plane into the western façade of the Pentagon in Arlington County, Virginia, at 9:37 a.m.

A fourth high-jacked airplane, United Airlines Flight 93, a Boeing 757 aircraft, departed Newark International Airport at 8:42 a.m. en route to San Francisco, with a crew of seven and 33 passengers, not including four hijackers, (possibly aiming for Camp David), crashed into a field in Stonybrook Township, near Shanksville Pennsylvania at 10:03 a.m.

In New York, the early morning office workers at the Twin Towers streamed out of the building as panicked pedestrians were pelted with burning debris. Some of the people jumped out broken windows, as rescue workers watched helplessly, some jumped from eighty stories high

About an hour after the attacks the one-hundred-ten story south tower crumbled down. Approximately 50,000 employees worked in the building for the 500 leading international companies that had offices in the World Trade Center. Thousands were feared dead.

As rescue workers were swarming in to evacuate the workers, the North tower came tumbling down, trapping firemen and rescue workers, falling to their death.

Also, Trade Center No. 7 collapsed later with an unknown number of people trapped inside.

They ran for their lives, bloodied and burned, hysterical and confused as they fled the burning building only to be engulfed in a tidal wave of toxic smoke and ash as the World Trade Center collapsed. As those caught in the tragedy ran to safety, around them were the bodies of victims who had jumped from upper floors to escape the inferno.

As an indication of the potential death toll, Mayor Rudolph Giuliani was asked whether the city has asked federal officials for 6,000 body bags. He replied "yes" that's correct.

Some of the passengers had cell phones and called their loved ones telling them what was taking place, each describing the same circumstances. They indicated the hi-jackers were armed with knives in some cases stabbing the flight attendants and then they took control of the planes. And then passengers said their last good-byes to their loved ones over their cell phones, as the fourth airplane crashed into the ground.

9/11 is the single deadliest terrorist attack in human history and the single deadliest incident for firefighters and law enforcement officers (that went into the blazing buildings in a hope to rescue the workers), in the history of the United States, with 343 and 72 fighters killed, respectively.

An amazing display of American flags, by Americans were flown across the country after the 9/11 attacks, while citizens showed their sorrow and support for the victims families. A "United We Stand" fund was raising large amounts of money to help the survivor's families that lost loved ones in all four of the hijacked airplane attacks.

September 18, 2001 –President Bush visited the badly damaged Pentagon. Bush said that the U. S. is ready to defend freedom at any cost, he said this as the Defense Department had already called-up orders for an estimated 35,000 reservists.

A defense military intelligence official blamed terror boss, Osama bin Laden to be behind the attacks. State and Federal officials secured the city to safe-guard the Nation. The White House was shut down and our President (Bush) rushed to safety.

The big question is, how did thirty-three terrorists seize control of four US passenger airplanes at three different airports, on the same morning, within a two-hour and forty-five-minute period, and **why** didn't the airports security detect them?

Three weeks before the attacks – Osama bin Laden, who emerged as a prime suspect, and is a Saudi exile who warned that he would carry out "an unprecedented attack" on the United States interest. The madman boasted he would strike against U. S. targets because of American support of Israel. He had made the threat in a statement passed to Abdel-Bari Atwan, editor of the London based Al-Quds al Arabi newspaper.

Bin Laden came to prominence fighting alongside the U. S. backed Afghan mujahedeen – holy warriors in their war against Soviet troops in the 1980's. Then he turned against the United States during the 1991 Gulf War, seething at the deployment of the U. S. troops in Saudi Arabia during the Gulf War Campaign to oust Iraq from Kuwait.

It was reported on 13 September 2001, that Federal authorities identified more than a dozen hijackers of Middle Eastern descent in Tuesday's bombings and gathered evidence linking them to Osama bin Laden and other terrorist networks, law enforcement officials said. Some of the suspects in the country are believed to have learned to fly commercial jetliners before the attacks. At least one hijacker on each of the planes was trained at a United States flight school. The hijackers used both cash and credit cards to purchase their plane tickets and hotel rooms.

AMERICA FIGHTS BACK – on 11 September 2001, President George W. Bush called on Afghanistan's leaders to hand over Osama bin Laden and other al Qaeda leaders and close their terrorist training camps. He also demanded the return of all detained foreign nationals and the opening of terrorist training sites to inspection.

Congress passed S. J. Resolution 23, "Authorization for Use of Military Force", on 14 September 2001, this bill was signed by President George W. Bush on 18 September 2001, and it authorized the President to use "all necessary and appropriate force against those nations, organizations, or persons he determined planned, authorized, committed, or aided the terrorist attacks that occurred on 11 September 2001, or harbor such organizations or persons.

CHAPTER EIGHTEEN

AFGHANISTAN

Taliban gunners in the Afghanistan capital released a thunderous barrage at the plane cruising high over Kabul on 6 October 2001, as President Bush delivered a stern warning that "time is running out" for the regime to hand over Osama bin Laden.

On 7 October, American and British forces unleashed air strikes against military targets and Osama bin Laden's training camps inside Afghanistan aiming at terrorists blamed for the September 11 attacks.

Tomahawk Cruise missiles and bombs found targets halfway around the globe as Bush announced "We Will Not Falter and We Will Not Fail".

Names of some of the other terrorists mentioned in the investigation as taking part in the 9/11 attacks were, Zacarias Moussaoui, Ramzi bin al-Shibh, Abu Turab al-Urduni, Mohammed Atef, Abu Dahdah, Mounir el-Motassadeq, Mohamed Atta, Marwan al-Shehhi, Ziad Jarrah, Ramzi bin al-Shibh and Said Bahaji.

In Osama bin Laden's "Letter to America", in November 2002, he explicitly stated that al-Qaeda's motives for their attacks included:

> US support of Israel
>
> US support for the "attacks against Muslims" in Somalia
>
> US support of Philippines against Muslims in the Moro conflict

US support for Israeli "aggression" against Muslims in Lebanon

US support of Russian "atrocities against Muslims" in Chechnya

Pro-American governments in the Middle East (who "act as your agents") being against Muslim interests.

US support of Indian "oppression against Muslims" in Kashmir

The presence of US troops in Saudi Arabia, and the sanctions against Iraq.

After evading capture for almost a decade, bin Laden was located in Pakistan and killed by SEAL Team Six of the U.S. Navy on May 1, 2011, during the Obama administration.

The question of could the 9/11 attacks have been avoided or detected will always remain a question through the ages, as in the case of the Pearl Harbor attacks on 7 December 1941.

It is fact that on 6 August 2001, the CIA's Presidential Daily Brief (PDB), designated "For the President Only", was entitled "bin Laden Determined to Strike in U. S. The memo noted that "The FBI information indicates patterns of suspicious activity in this country consistent with preparations for hijackings or other types of attacks".

In mid-August, one Minnesota flight school alerted the FBI about Zacarias Moussaoui, who had asked "suspicious questions." The request to search his laptop was denied by FBI headquarters due to the lack of probable cause. However, he was arrested for overstaying his French visa.

In 2002, February 12th, former Yugoslav President Slobodan Milosevic goes on trial charged with sixty-six counts of genocide and war crimes in Bosnia, Croatia and Kosovo.

Khalid Sheikh Mohammed – was arrested on 1 March 2003 in Pakistan, by Pakistan security officials working with the CIA. During the US hearings at Guantanamo Bay, March 2007, Mohammed confessed his responsibility for the attacks, stating he "was responsible for the 9/11 operation from A to Z and that his statement was not under duress".

As of this date, Saturday, 15 February 2020, we still have troops in Afghanistan, but according to today's newspaper, the United States and the Taliban have reached agreement on a temporary truce that will take effect in the coming days and, if successfully completed, will lead to a formal cease-fire and the ultimate withdraw of American troops from Afghanistan after serving there for eighteen years, since the September 11, 2001, terrorist attacks.

CHAPTER NINETEEN

SECOND IRAQI WAR

The war, also called the Persian Gulf War, on 20 March 2003, a second war between Iraq and a U.S.- led coalition began, this time with the stated U. S. objective of removing Saddam Hussein from power, and ostensibly, finding and destroying weapons of mass destruction.

In 1979, Saddam Hussein became President of Iraq. In the early days of his party Iraq used its vast oil wealth to build schools, dams, and highways. Its health system was the pride of the Middle East, and a middle class bloomed.

The irony of Iraq is it could have become a rich, progressive nation instead of a ravaged outcast. If Saddam had been liable and not planned for those foolish acts, Iraq could be the aspiration of the Arab world.

In 1980, still in his first year as ruler of Iraq, Hussein invaded Iran, his own neighbor, apparently hoping to gain more territory. That war ended with at least 150,000 Iraqis dead. Two years later he invaded Kuwait.

By February 2003, nearly seventy-five percent of Iraqis lived on government food rations, at least one-third of the children under five suffered from malnutrition. And the childhood death rate doubled in the past ten years.

The refusing to comply with the United Nations in not destroying his weapons of mass destruction has caused many nations unrest.

Those that have studied him stop short of calling him crazy. They call him, brutal, a cunning man, whose basic instincts never have been restrained. His biggest flaw is the thirst for power.

Also in February 2003, while the U.S. was pressuring Iraq to destroy its weapons of mass destruction and threatening war against the Iraq's, other countries were protesting.

Several million demonstrators took to the streets on five continents in a wave of mostly peaceful protest against the proposal of a U. S. - led war against Iraq. The largest rallies were in Rome, London, Berlin and Paris. Rome turned out more than 1 million protesters alone.

In late January 2003, the Bush Administration moved toward a military showdown with Iraq, after U. N. inspectors credited Iraq with limited cooperation in search for weapons.

The Pentagon placed 150,000 troops and four aircraft carrier battle groups, each with more than 70 warplanes in the Persian Gulf region by the end of February 2003. Colin Powell, Secretary of State during the Bush administration urged the United Nations Security Council (UNSC) to move against Saddam because Iraq has failed to disarm, harbors terrorists, and hides behind a "web of lies".

The middle of March 2003, President Bush and summit partners from Britain and Spain gave the U.N. a deadline of one week to endorse the use of force to compel Iraq's immediate disarmament.

Once again, the opponents of war on Iraq joined in a global vigil. In Cinnaminson, New Jersey, on Route 130, they held candles and hoped that their presence would send an antiwar message to the cars racing by.

The candlelight vigil was part of the global vigil for peace held around the world on Sunday, 17 March 2003. It is documented that more than 6,700 vigils in 140 countries were scheduled.

As the threats of war were apparent, in Northern Iraq, people were fleeing for fear of attacks from Hussein's forces in the event of a U. S. led- war on Iraq.

On 18 March 2003, Saddam Hussein mocked an American ultimatum to surrender power, and the Bush Administration claimed public support from 30 nations for its supporting Iraq's disarmament.

Thursday, 20 March 2003, IRAQ'S WAR BEGINS – Washington, United States Forces launched air strikes against "targets" of military importance in Iraq with cruise missiles and precision-guided bombs against a site near Baghdad where Iraq leaders were thought to be. The strikes used Tomahawk cruise missiles and precision-guided bombs dropped from F-117 Nighthawks, the Air Forces Stealth fighter-bombers.

As Bush gave the order to attack – tank crews from Alpha Company, 4th Battalion, 64th Regiment, prayed during a heavy sandstorm near the Iraqi border in Kuwait.

The United States officials again tried to talk the Iraqi regime into giving up. American and Britain combat units rumbled across the desert into Iraq from the south and bombed limited targets in Baghdad, but withheld the massive onslaught.

It's now the 2nd day of April and the Pentagon doesn't know whether Saddam Hussein is dead or alive. As the battle in Iraq is becoming a shooting war on the ground.

It's a bloody grind of street fights, ambushes and unpleasant surprises as the American forces near the gates of Baghdad.

Early April, Spring 2003, Kirkuk, Iraq with a slumming speed of barely a fight, Kirkuk and its oil fields changed hands as statues of Saddam Hussein lay broken in the dust.

During 15 April, U.S. troops swept through Saddams hometown and began disarming residents as the Marines came under fire while seizing an airstrip on the towns' outskirts. The troops also set up barriers to prevent Saddam and his leaders from escaping. His Presidential Palace was also seized without a fight.

Allies begin leaving Baghdad – On 20 April 2003, one month after the first attacks on Iraq, the military presence in Baghdad lightened when the Marines left and the Army was in control to stabilize the capital. Retired Lt. Gen. Jay Garner arrived in Iraq as the country's postwar administrator to restore power and water. Garner, said that he has no intention of leading Iraqi and that the new ruler is going to be an Iraqi.

In the heart of Iraq's capital, Defense Secretary, Donald H. Rumsfeld addressed a crowd with a reassuring message to the people. Iraq belongs to you, he said. The coalition has no intention of owning or running Iraq.

On 1 May, 2003, President Bush, aboard the USS Abraham Lincoln said that the United States and our allies have prevailed against Saddam Hussein and will comfort any nation tied to terrorists, and that major combat in Iraq has ended. Also, that much work is still to be done, including bringing order to the country, finding weapons of mass destruction, creating an Iraq government, and punishing leaders of the fallen regime, including Saddam.

Nine requests for initial reconstruction work in Iraq had been issued by USAID, (United States Agency for International Development). Three contracts had been awarded for a total of $19.7 million.

Like many countries, the United States ties most of its aid to U.S. goods and companies. After criticism from British companies, USAID has said foreign companies can take part as subcontractors.

A contract was awarded to Research Triangle Institute, to seek and maximize Iraqi participation in all phases and aspects of the reconstruction as the transition to Iraqi administration occurs, awarded $7.9 million.

Seaport Administration was awarded $4.8 million on 24 March to Seattle-based Stevedoring Services of America.

International Resources Group awarded $7 million for personal support helping USAID in planning and managing reconstruction projects.

As of the above date the following companies were pending; 1. Capital Construction Emergency repair of electrical supply; water and sanitation systems; roads and bridges; public buildings, irrigation structures and port upgrades. 2. Airport Administration Management of humanitarian and transshipment operations by air. 3. Theater Logistical Support, warehousing customs clearance, trucking and provision of bottled water. 4. Public Health, help to restore the public health service. 5. Primary and Secondary Education, assistance in upgrading schools, printing textbooks and training teachers. 6. Iraq Community Action Program, twelve month program to promote diverse and representative citizen participation in and among impoverished communities throughout Iraq.

On 22 July, Saddam's sons Odoi and Qusai died in a blaze of gunfire when U.S. forces stormed a palatial villa in Northern Iraq.

In August of the same year Iraq resumed pumping oil from its Northern fields for the first time since the war.

On Thursday, 27 November 2003, President Bush flew to Baghdad to spend Thanksgiving with US troops and thanked them for defending the American people from danger.

On 13th December 2003, at 2:50 a.m., the United States intelligence received a tip about Saddam Hussein's whereabouts. At 12:36 p.m., Hussein was found at the bottom of a hole near a farmhouse.

5:14 a.m. Sunday, President Bush addressed the nation, telling the nation that Saddam Hussein was pulled out from a hole and that he surrendered without a shot. That he was being protected by two guards, and that troops confiscated $750,000 in cash and weapons.

DONALD H. RUMSFELD - History has it written that my next warrior, Donald H. Rumsfeld, served our country well. He is a graduate of Princeton University, Princeton, NJ, USA. He has degrees in political science, and after serving in the United States Navy for three years, at the age of thirty years old, in 1962, won a seat with the 13th Congressional District in Illinois, and was elected to the U. S. House of Representatives; he was elected by a large majority in 1964, 66, and 68 also. And as the sun comes creeping through the window over my desk in my study, I will attempt to tell the story of this great American gentleman.

Rumsfeld during his time in Congress

In 1969, President Nixon appointed Donald Rumsfeld to head the Office of Economic Opportunity (OEO) during which time Rumsfeld hired Frank Carlucci and Dick Chaney to serve under him. He also headed the Economic Stabilization Program, plus other programs and committee appointments.

Rumsfeld left OEO in 1970, when President Nixon named him Counselor to the President, a general advisory position that regularly interacted with the Nixon Administration.

In 1973, Donald Rumsfeld left Washington to serve as United States Ambassador to the North Atlantic Treaty Organization (NATO) in Brussels, Belgium. He served as the U.S. Permanent Representative of the North Atlantic Council and the Defense Planning Committee, and Nuclear Planning Group.

In August 1974, after President Richard Nixon resigned in the aftermath of the Watergate scandal, Donald Rumsfeld was called back to Washington to serve as transition chairman for the new President, Gerald Ford. Ford appointed him "White House Chief of Staff" when he served from 1974-75.

When Ford lost the election Rumsfeld returned to private business and was named CEO of the pharmaceutical corporation, G. D. Searle & Company. He was later named CEO of General Instrument from 1990 to 1993 and chairman of Gilead Sciences from 1997 to 2001.

During which time he continued part-time public service in various posts. In November 1983, he was appointed Special Envoy to the Middle East by President Ronald Reagan when Iraq and Iran were fighting. The U.S. wanted the conflict to end, and Rumsfeld was sent to the Middle East to serve as a mediator on behalf of the President.

In 2001, Donald Rumsfeld was named Secretary of Defense soon after President Bush took office. Rumsfeld's second tenure as Secretary of Defense cemented him as the most powerful Pentagon chief since Robert McNamara.

Following the 9/11 attacks, Rumsfeld led the military planning and execution of the U. S. Invasion of Afghanistan and the subsequent 2003 invasion of Iraq.

Rumsfeld's Invasion of Baghdad was with such lighting, in well under a month with very few American Casualties. Some far left wing officials criticized Rumsfeld's plan for the invasion, insisting that there were not enough troops and supplies and that it took too long to execute. President Bush stated in a news report that he would stand by Rumsfeld as Defense Secretary for the length of his term as President. On 8 November, 2006, President Bush announced that Rumsfeld would resign his position as Secretary of Defense.

Throughout his time as defense secretary, Rumsfeld was noted for his candor and quick wit when giving weekly press conferences or speaking with the press.

Rumsfeld has been awarded 11 honorary degrees. Following his years as CEO, president, and later chairman of G. D. Searle & Company, he was recognized as outstanding CEO in the pharmaceutical industry by the Wall Street Transcript (1980) and Financial World (1981).

Some of his other awards include:

All Navy Wrestling Champion (1956)

The Presidential Medal of Freedom (with Distinction) by President Ford (1977)

George C. Marshall Medal by Association of the U.S. Army (1984)

Woodrow Wilson Medal by Princeton University (1985)

Dwight D. Eisenhower Medal (1993)

Lone Sailor Award by U.S. Navy Memorial Foundation (2002)

Statesmanship Award by the United States Association of Former Members of Congress (2003)

Ronald Reagan Freedom Award (2003)

James H. Doolittle Award by the Hudson Institute (2003)

Gerald R. Ford Medal presented by President Ford and the Ford Foundation (2004)

Distinguished Eagle Scout Award by the Boy Scouts of America

Grand Cross of the Order of Merit of the Republic of Poland (2005)

Golden Raspberry Award for Worst Supporting Actor (2004) for his appearance on Fahrenheit 9/11

Union League of Philadelphia Gold Medal for Citizenship (2006)

Claremont Institute Statesmanship Award (2007)

Victory of Freedom Award from the Richard Nixon Foundation (2010)

Order of Anthony Wayne from Valley Forge Military Academy

Special Grand Cordon of the Order of Brilliant Star (2011, Republic of China)

National Flag award from Albania's President Bujar Nishani (2013)

Grand Cordon of the Order of the Rising Sun (2015)

Donald Rumsfeld's book, entitled "Known and Unknown A Memoir", was released on 8 February 2011.

Iraq after the 2003 Invasion: Soon after the 2003 invasion ended and before the new Iraq government was able to organize, a revolution started in Iraq that lasted until 2011.

In 2011 after the United States withdrew from the insurgents in Iraq, a new wave of anti-government engulfed Iraq. In 2012 thousands of casualties caused concern of a new civil war.

The rebels in Iraq consist of a mixture of foreign fighters, Iraqi units or mixtures of militias composing of over one dozen different military units, divided into a number of smaller cells, all opposing the American Multi Forces.

Iraq is one of the most unstable countries in the Middle East today, because of devastating wars, political divisions and very high unemployment.

In 2017-18, multinational military operations led by the United States against the terrorist groups in Iraq intensified. Then the Prime Minister Haider al-Abadi declared that the Islamic State of Iraq and the Levant (ISIL) were driven out of the country for the last time.

When the government was run by Prime Minister Haider al-Abadi, a Shiite, and a strong leader for Iraq, it was kept together. The federal government is a coalition of Shiite, Sunni, Kurdish, and other leaders.

In October 2018 Prime Minister Adil Abdul-Mahdi al Muntafiki took over office and anti-government protests took place in Iraq. Again in 2019 protesting Iraq's influence in the country more than 500 protesters were killed and approximately 19,000 wounded.

In November 2019, due to the unrest of protesters Abdul-Mahdi was dismissed as Prime Minister, but he remains in a Warder Guard/Caretaker capacity.

On 3 January 2020, U. S. President Donald Trump ordered the drone-strike assassination of the Iranian commander Qassem Soleimani and Iraq military leader Abu Mahdi al-Muhandis and eight others at the Baghdad airport. No one was hurt at the bases, but in the confusion a Ukrainian civilian passenger jet was destroyed by one of the missiles, killing 176 people.

CHAPTER TWENTY

IRAQ'S BEGINNING CIVILIAZATION

Iraq's people have been fighting for many, thousands of years. And the Iraqi people have one of the earliest regions of civilizations. Archaeologists digging deep beneath the floor of the high-vaulted natural cave of Shanidar, on a southward-facing slope of the Zagros Mountains in northern Iraq, have discovered remains indicating that an adult Neanderthal man lived there some 45,000 years ago. Digging deeper they found the bones of another adult who lived about 60,000 years ago, and still deeper they found a year-old baby who lived 70,000 years ago.

By 3500 B.C. Southern Mesopotamia had become a land of city-states with a common Sumerian culture. One of these city-states was Ur, also known as Ur of the Chaldees, and identified in the Bible as the home of Abraham.

In succeeding centuries Ur came under the control of a Semitic Babylonian dynasty, was captured, destroyed and rebuilt several times by various kings and invaders, and apparently declined some time during the fourth century B.C., for its name then disappears from historical records. The city lay buried and forgotten under a mound of sand until its location was re-discovered in the nineteenth century.

About 2100 B.C., Hammurabi, a Semitic king, established his capital in the hitherto unimportant city of Babylon. He was a warrior who extended his empire into northern Iraq but was known as a lawgiver.

Hanging Gardens of Babylon - Although Babylon became wealthy and powerful from commerce; it was destroyed by the Assyrians. Its great period came later, after the city had been built, and its most brilliant era was under Nebuchadnezzar an enthusiastic builder. He created a beautiful city with fortified walls and magnificent palaces and temples on both sides of the Euphrates River. The royal palace with many arches was of brick lavishly decorated in vivid hues, and high above it were the official gardens of the king, known as the Hanging Gardens of Babylon.

In 539 B.C., however, the last of the Babylonian rulers surrendered to Cyrus the Great, and Babylon became a minor town in the Persian Empire. Its downfall is attributed by some to the selfish unconcern of the rich, by others to excessive spending on lavish palaces.

Assyrians - Meanwhile the Assyrians, another Semitic group, had founded about 3000 B.C. the city of Assur in what is now Northern Iraq. By 1300 B.C. they had established a powerful empire stretching from the Persian Gulf to the Mediterranean Sea. They were famed for their military bravery over all. Their last king, Assur-bani-pal, (approximately 669-626 B.C.), compiled at Nineveh, the learning of the day, into thousands of clay tablets, thus, creating one of the earliest of the world's libraries.

One of the Assyrian government's most prominent achievements was the establishment of a permanent military force, to fight its endless wars. It subjected defeated people to occupation, for many men were needed for all agriculture and food had to be imported. Also the methods used were among the cruelest in the ancient world. The system eventually led the Assyrians themselves and the conquered people to revolt not once but again and again. In 606 B.C. Scythians, nomadic conquerors from the north shore of the Black Sea (now in the U.S.S.R.), destroyed Nineveh, and Assyrian power was extinguished.

When Cyrus the Great captured Babylon in 539, Semitic rule in Iraq came to an end. The leadership then was taken over by the Indo-Europeans, and for the next 1,200 years Iraq were under the rule of first the Persians, then the Greeks under Alexander the Great, then the Seleucians, the Parthian Persians, and finally the Sassanian Persians (226-637 A. D.). As part of the Persian Empire, Iraq was repeatedly overrun in the contest between Persia and Rome that went on for several hundred years – and suffered accordingly. The Persians, Greeks and Romans were followed by the Arabs, a newly emerging force from the heart of Arabia. The Arabs brought with them a new language, Arabic, and a new religion, Islam, which have profoundly influenced Iraq ever since.

Golden Age - In 750 one family, descended from Abbas, the uncle of Mohammed, had gained control and a few years later established its capital in Iraq, at Baghdad. This was the beginning of a Golden Age, which lasted more or less until 1258. It was ruler Mansur who proceeded to build a new city, on the west bank of the Euphrates River, which within thirty years had become one of the largest in the Mediterranean world. A city of great places and gardens, and one of the wealthiest cities in the world, exchanging ambassadors and trading with many lands, buying silks and porcelains from China, spices from India, and gold and ivory from East Africa. The era of wealth and grandeur is reflected in the "Thousand and One Nights". You may remember that Scheherazade kept her husband from killing her by telling these stories to him over 1,001 nights; by which time he had apparently decided he enjoyed her company. Among the best-known stories are those which recount the adventures of Ali Baba, Sinbad the Sailor and Aladdin.

The following centuries the Abbas sides had several ups and downs. The Turks, who were brought in as slaves to man the regular military forces gradually came to occupy high places in government, weakening and dividing it still further. The beginning of the end was the takeover during the Mongol invasion in 1258.

Within a few days Hulagu (grandson of Genghis Khan) and his hordes descended upon Baghdad, killed Nasir, the ruler at the time and tens of thousands of its citizens, burned and looted shops and palaces and overrun the country-side, crippling industry and commerce and lay in waste the irrigation canals and dams indispensable in this dry land.

The darkest period for Iraq was followed by other invasions from abroad, and ended with conquest by the Turks in 1543; they ruled Iraq until just after the end of World War I.

From 1920 to 1932, British Mandate efforts came to be recognized as valuable contributions to the nation, they stabilized an acceptable constitution, a parliament and monarchy (King Faisal) was created, and an efficient government was established.

By 1932, when the British withdrew, the revenue from oil already amounted to one-quarter of the entire national income, after the death of King Faisal in 1933, there was a series of national uprisings culminating in the Revolution of 1958 which overthrew the monarchy and proclaimed Iraq a republic. In 1964, once again the government was overthrown and a new Cabinet was formed.

As this will give my readers a sense of what the United States is dealing with as far as the Country of Iraq is concerned; they have been a fighting country since its beginning and perhaps will always be. What I don't understand is why we have to send our military troops over to other countries to get killed or wounded in an endless war. In reality, the Iraq's don't want the United States there.

THE END

SOURCES

As I researched the veterans military history for my three published books, "A Salute to Our Veterans", I had accumulated over three hundred military works and read almost all of them. While doing the reading and researching, I made index notes of special actions that I had read about, and doing so, I was able to go back to my many notes for information while writing this book.

Other sources that I give attribution to are newspapers that I have collected over the years, such as the "Daily News", a New York newspaper, I have several dated from September of 1940, when Germany was raiding the British forces, before the bombing of Pearl Harbor, and some date to early 1942, when our soldiers were in country and the Japanese were sinking U.S. ships and U.S. subs were fighting back.

I credit Wikipedia for most of the information about the early England forces during the fifteen hundreds and some of the most recent reference I obtained due the fact that not many books have been published about whats going on in Asia and the Persian Gulf. I credit the Burlington County Times Newspapers that I had collected, a New Jersey based newspaper for the information for a more accurate guide about what happened during the attacks on September 11, (9/11).

Needless to note that this book is mostly based on other published sources and from the many veterans that I had the opportunity to interview and that they gave me detailed information about their military experiences. And I especially thank the veterans that gave me permission to include there military history in this book.

Irene Jean Dumas-Gammon
April 2020

INDEX

A

Adams, John 23
Adams, Samuel 22
Afghanistan, 149-152
Alamogordo, New Mexico 73
Allied Expeditionary Forces 62
Americas 03
American Air Lines 146
American Revolutio 10
Amtrak's 71
Andersonville Conf. Prison 25
An Khe, Vietnam 110-111, 117
Annam 102-03
Arizona 17
Arlington National Cemetery 90
Asia 91, 101-109
Austria-Hungary 31

B

Baghdad 154-56
Baker, James A. III 131
Bataan 51
Bataan Death March 51
Battle of the Argonne Forest 36
Battle of the Bridges 135
Battle of the Bulge 67
Battle of Wounded Knee 30
Beauregard (confederate) 27
Beirut 128-29
Belgium 157
Ben Hai River 102
Bockscar 61
Booth, John Wilkes 25
Bora, Bora 53
Bosque Redondo Reservation 19
Bradley, Omar 63, 68, 70
Braun, Eva 70
British 32-35, 40-46, 50-52, 64-69
British Royal Navy 44

Brown, Joe E. 89
Brown, John 20-21
Buddhists103-04, 109
Bush, George 132-38,143-48, 158
Butterfield, Daniel, Brig. Gen. (Union Army) 23

C

California 18, 56
Calley, Lt. Wm. Jr. 121
Camp Bradford 55
Camp Lejeune 139-40
Camp Pendleton 56
Cambodia 102-04
Cam Rhan Bay 110
Canada 14
Cape Good Hope 05
Cape Verde Islands 04
Capone, Al 43
Catholics103
Cemetery Hill 23-24
Chain Kai Shek 92
Channel Islands 47
Cherbourg, France 62-65
Cherokee Indians 08
Cherokee Wars 08
Chesapeake 13
China 51, 101-105, 163
Chosen Reservoir 95-96
Church, Major General John H. 97-99
Churchill, Sir Winston 46-51, 62-64, 76, 83
Cluska Mountains 17
Clark, General 68
Cloud Pass 102
Cochin, China 102
Collins, Joe, General 60
Concentration Camps
    Belsen, (torture house) 69

Chelmno (extermination) 45
Dachau 86
Mooseburg 69
Ravensbruck prison 45
Corregidor (Philippines) 51
Custer, General 112

D

DaNang, Vietnam 103-07
Davis, Jefferson (Con. President), 20-23
Dayton Accords 143
Dayton Peace Accords 143
DeGaulle, Pres. France 103
Dien Bien Phu 115
Doolittle, James Lt. Col. (WWII pilot),
Drake, Elizabeth 04
Drake, Sir Francis 02-06

E

Eisenhower, Dwight D. (US Pres.) 62-69. 74-78
England 1-10, 22-47, 62-82
English Channel 35
English Colonies 10
Enola Gay. (The B-17 that dropped The Atomic Bomb on Japan) 61
European Theatre 51-55

F

Finland 45
Florida (NSVA 108, 114, 119, 121, 125
Ford's Theatre 25
Fort Sumter 22, 29
France 31
French 7-9

G

Gammon, Kenneth, Lt. (Vietnam Vet.) 108, 173
Garofalo, Joseph (WW II veteran) 55-61
Geneva Accords 126

Geneva Conference 102
Geneva Convention 76
Germans 63-68
Germantown 16
Germany 63-68
Grenada 130-31
Gettysburg Address 24
Gold Beach (Normandy) 64
Golden Hine (flag ship) 03
Gothic Line 67
Grand Anse Campus 131
Grant, Ulysses S (General, Civil War) 22-26
Green, Nathanael, Major. Gen. (Rev. War) 15
Guadalcanal 53-55
Guantanamo Bay 151
Giuliani, Rudolph (NY Mayor) 147
Gulf War 134-148

H

Harlem Hellfighters 40
Harpers Ferry 21
Hawkins, John 03
Henry Cabot Lodge 106
Heydrich, Richard 44
Hill #1419 95
Hill #1542 95
Hiroshima, Japan 61
Hitler, Adolf 44, 89
Ho Chi Minh (leader of N. Viennese) 102-03
Hodges, Courtney 63
Hoffman, Brig. Gen 25
Hoffmann, Johanna 47
Hue, Vietnam 102-114
Hussein, Sadden 135-45

I

Inchon, Korea 94
Independence Missouri 33-34
Indians 08, 17-19, 30
International Military Tribunals 87
Indochina 100

Iran 129
Iran-Iraq War 126-27, 134-37
Iraq 142-45
Italy 71
Iwo Jima 71

J

James 1 (King) 06
Japanese War Trials 87
John, Rick (Navy Seabee) 120-21
Johnson, Andrew (U.S. President) 25
Juno Beach (Normandy) 64

K

Kamikazes 71
Karadzic, Radovan, (Bosnian Pres.) 143-44
Keitel, Wilhelm, (Ger. Field Marshall) 70
Kennedy, John F. (US President) 103-06
Khe Shan (Vietnam) 115
Khrushchev, Soviet Premier 99
King, Ernest, (USN Admiral) 50
King, Martin Luther (reg. preacher). 119
Korea 91-100, 107, 125
Kraft, Howard (WW 1 veteran) 33-40
Kurdistan 144
Kuwait (Asia) 134-143

L

Laden, Osama bin 148-51
Laos (Southeast Asia) 99
Lawrence, Lord Justice (presided over Nuremburg trials 79
League of Nations 42
Lebanese National Army (LNA) 129
Lebanon (Middle East) 129
Lee, Robert E. (Conf. Officer 21-22
Leyte Gulf 72
Lidice, Czechoslovakia 44-45
Lincoln, Abraham (U.S. President) 21-26
Little Bighorn 112
Littlefield, Catharine 15
Lusitania 31
Luxembourg 46, 66

M

MacArthur, General 51, 73-74,
McAuliffe, Tony, General 67
McCollum, Author, Lt. Gen. 48
Mein Kampf 42
Mekong River 103
Military Asst. Advisory Group (MAAG) 105
Milosevic, Slobodan (president of Serbia) 144
Mitchell, William, Brig. Gen., 42
Mladic, Ralko, (Bosnia General) 143
Mohammed, Khalid (Sheikh) 150
Montgomery, Bernard (British Army General, Field Marshal) 75-76
Moreell, Ben (US Navy Admiral) 52
Mulberries 64-65
Multi National Force (MNF) 67
Mussolini, Benito (Prime Minister of Italy during WW II) 43
My Lai Massacre (Vietnam) 121

N

Nagasaki, Japan 61, 73
Nancy, France 36
Narbona, (Indian Chief- New .Mexico) 19
Navajo Indians19
National Socialist Party 80-85
Navy Seabees 120
Newman, Mary 04
Ngo Dinh Diem 102
Nimitz, Chester W. (US Navy Admiral) 73
Nine-Eleven 146-158
Nixon, Richard (US President)157
Noriega, Manuel (Panama dictator) 132
Normandy Invasion 62, 75, 89

169

North Atlantic Treaty Organization (NATO) 43
North Korea 94-99
North Vietnam 102, 122
Norton, Oliver Wilcox (bugler) 23
Norway, 44
Nuremberg Trials (trials of the Germans) 70-82
Nurse Carvell (Edith Louisa-British nurse) 31

O

Okinawa (military base during WW II) 71-72
Omaha Beach (Normandy Invasion) 64
Operation- Delaware, 112, 116
    Desert Shield, 134
    Desert Storm, 128-136
    Glory 97
    Jed Stuart (TET Offensive) 113
    Just Cause 132-136
    Menu 122
    Over Lord 74

P

Pegasus 1115
Urgent Fury 130
Pacific Ocean 49
Palace of Justice (Nuremburg, Ger.) 78
Palestine Liberation Org. 128
Panama 132-133
Panama Canal 132
Patton, Gen. George S, Jr. 65, 76 WWII
Pearl Harbor, Hawaii 151
Pentagon, US Dept. of Defense 146-48, 154
Pershing, John J. (US Army General) 32, 74
Persian Gulf 134-137, 154-162
Pfremmer, Kent (USAF Chief) 123-25
Phillip III of Spain 06
Philadelphia 11

Poland 44
Polk, James Knox (11th Pres. US) 18
Port of Dunkirk-battle WWI 46
Port of Hungnam (evacuation site) 95
Port Hueneme (USN Seabees base) 56
Port of Pusan, So. Korea 94
Potomac River (battle of Civil War) 19
Potsdam Conference 92
Pusan Perimeter 94, 97
Pyle, Ernie (war-time correspondent) 72

Q

Queen Elizabeth 02-06
Queen Victoria 22

R

Reed, Carl (US POW-WWII), prologue
Regan, Ronald (US President) 132
Republic of Korea 97
Rhine River (Germany) 68
Ridgeway, Gen. (US Army) 96
Roosevelt, Eleanor (First Lady) 48-52
Roosevelt, Franklin D. 48-89
Rosie the Riveter (WW II) 52
Royal Air Force (British) 55
Rumsfeld, Donald H. 155-58
Russia 68-70, 89

S

Saigon, Vietnam 102-126
Sand Creek, Colorado 18
Sarajevo (Cap. City in Bosnia 143
Saudi Arabia 134-148
Savannas, Georgia 29
Schwarzkopf, Norman, Gen. 134-140
Seabees (US Navy) 52-54, 107-08
Second Continental Congress 16
Seminary Ridge 2 3
Seoul Korea 94
Shenandoah 11
Shanksville, PA 147
Shaba Lebanese Camp 128
Shatia Lebanese Camp 128

Sherman, William Tecumseh, General 25-30
Shields, Marvin G. (US Navy Seabee-Medal of Honor Recp.) 108
Ships-Bismarck (Battleship) 90
    USS Indianapolis (heavy cruiser) 72
    USS Missouri (Battleship) 73
    USS Ruben James (Destroyer WW II) 48
    Sultana (Steamship) 25-26
    USS Wayne (Attack-Transport, WW II) 56
Sieber, Etta (WW II German prisoner) 47
Skipper, Charles (US Army, Vietnam) 110-119
Skipper, S. Sgt. Kathryn A. Gates-USMC), 138-42
Sioux Indians 30
Sir Walter Raleigh ((British warrior) 04
Soldiers National Cemetery 24
South East Asia Treaty Organization 104-8
South Korea 91-98
South Vietnam 102-122
Soviet Union 122-134
Sprayberry, Michael (Medal of Honor Recp.) 119
Stalin, Joseph (Russian Communist dictator) 45, 92
Superfortress 73
Sweden 45-46
Sweeney, Charles W. (USAF - World War Two) 73
Sword Beach 64
Syngman Rhee (So. Korean President) 92, 97

T

Taliban 150-52
TET Offensive 113-14
Texas 17-18
The Tin Cup Trip 136

Thirteen Colonies 13-14
Thirty-Eighth Parallel 92
Tibbett's, Paul W. Jr. (USAF pilot-WW II) 73
Tinian Island 73
Tokyo Bay 73
Tonkin Annan 102
Treaty of London 06
Treaty of Nonsuch 02
Treaty of Paris 14
Trenton, NJ16, 173
Tripoli 17, 38-39, 62
True Blue Campus 130
Truman, Harry S. 33rd Presto US 68, 79, 91
Trump, Donald (45th Pres. of US) 160
Tunisia, 128
Turner, Richard (V. Admiral) 71
Tuskegee Airmen 48
Twin Towers 147

U

Union Army 22-28
United Air Lines (Ft. 175) 146
United Airlines (Ft. 93) 146
United Nations Sec. Council 145
United States Agency for International Developments (USAID) 1255-56
United States Civil War 29
U. S. Dakotas 66
Utah Beach (Normandy) 64

V

Versailles Treaty 79
V-Bombs 65
Vienna 42, 86, 104
Viet Cong 106-121
Vietnam War 101-127
Vietnam Women's Memorial, 121

W

Wax's (Women Army Corps) 53
Wall (The National Vietnam Veterans Memorial), 127

Washington, George (First U.S. President 13-14
Wilson, Woodrow (28th Pres. of U.S.) 31
Wolf's Lair 70
World War One 31-42, 74
World War Two 44-88
Wounded Knee Battle 30
World Trade Center (Manhattan) 146-47

IRENE J. DUMAS is a retired author of a pamphlet, printed and stapled in 2004 titled, Veterans and Still Rollin, which she wrote after interviewing twenty-nine veterans and learning their military history at a skating rink where she skated.

Inspired by the reaction of the veterans, Irene continued interviewing veterans and to her credit has written three books, after interviewing over 180 veterans, all three books are titled "A Salute to Our Veterans", with different sub-titles, published by Trafford, and are in the Library of Congress. After learning volumes of military history she wrote this book "Century's of War's".

Although she was born and raised in Trenton, New Jersey, Irene moved to Florida in 2004 on 30 March 2012, Irene married her second husband, Kenneth D. Gammon and now lives in Lakeland, Florida.